identity CRISIS

"To walk through a crisis is the journey none of us ever chooses. But if you or someone you love is making that journey, there is no better guide than the wisdom of one who has gone before you. Joy Anisa is just such a wise guide and this book is filled with the lessons she is graciously passing back to us all. Full of integrity, Joy has walked from crisis to credibility. Let her gentle spirit come alongside you and show you the way."

—**Angela Thomas**, Best-selling author and speaker

"Everyone should read this book to learn about crisis and what it means to find hope through it. Joy Anisa presents a well-studied, Christ-centered look at a life saturated with crisis, and how one can discover healing and growth. With compassion, she points readers to one ultimate truth: It all comes back to Jesus. This book is a practical guide for effective ministry and personal growth."

—**Brody Holloway**, Director, Snowbird Wilderness Outfitters

"When the landscape of your life changes and you are left standing in ruins, Joy Anisa points you to the master Contractor and will walk beside you as you allow Christ to rebuild your life brick by brick."

—**Pastor Johnny Hunt, Sr.** Pastor,
First Baptist Church Woodstock, GA

identity
CRISIS

Moving From Crisis to CREDIBILITY

joy anisa

NEW YORK

identity CRISIS
Moving From Crisis to CREDIBILITY

Published in New York, New York, by Morgan James Publishing. Morgan James and The Entrepreneurial Publisher are trademarks of Morgan James, LLC. www.MorganJamesPublishing.com

The Morgan James Speakers Group can bring authors to your live event. For more information or to book an event visit The Morgan James Speakers Group at www.TheMorganJamesSpeakersGroup.com.

BitLit
FOR ALL THE BOOKS YOU OWN

FREE eBook edition for your existing eReader with purchase

PRINT NAME ABOVE

For more information, instructions, restrictions, and to register your copy, go to **www.bitlit.ca/readers/register** or use your QR Reader to scan the barcode:

ISBN 978-1-61448-915-3 paperback
ISBN 978-1-61448-916-0 eBook
ISBN 978-1-61448-918-4 hardcover
Library of Congress Control Number: 2013948160

Cover Design by:
Rachel Lopez
www.r2cdesign.com

Interior Design by:
Bonnie Bushman
bonnie@caboodlegraphics.com

In an effort to support local communities, raise awareness and funds, Morgan James Publishing donates a percentage of all book sales for the life of each book to Habitat for Humanity Peninsula and Greater Williamsburg.

Get involved today, visit
www.MorganJamesBuilds.com.

Habitat for Humanity
Peninsula and
Greater Williamsburg
Building Partner

Dedication

There will never be an adequate thank you to the women who have walked with me through the devastation of my crisis. Kristy—for taking every step with me and keeping me focused on the One who brings true healing. Michelle—for loving me as only a big sister can love and for making sure I kept a balanced perspective. O'Nealya—for all the tears you cried with me and the many hours of reminding me of God's unbreakable promises. Jeanette—for the gift of your wisdom and the tender compassion you pour over my life. Only heaven knows the hours you sat before the Father on my behalf. Maria—for the times you unselfishly prayed over me and for me. Each of you has carried my burdens to the only One who could take on such a heavy task, and I dedicate this book to you.

Table of Contents

Foreword

I first met Joy in 2006, in a Bible study at a church where my husband was interviewing for a ministry position. Several people spoke during the discussion time, but she stood out to me because of her insight.

We ended up taking the position and moving to the town where she had lived her whole life. We joined their life group and I will never forget the day she came to us (new people, in unfamiliar surroundings, and far away from home) and said, "I want to keep your kids for you, because I know you don't have any family here." It turned out she was not only insightful, but considerate and compassionate.

From there we became fast friends. We shared a strong affinity for sarcasm, an interest in psychology, a calling to minister to women, and many, many pots of coffee. And while we always laughed together and talked (A LOT!) we had something few people find or maintain in relationships: accountability. Joy was never afraid to *speak the truth in love.*

Besides telling me when I was wrong, she also readily admitted her own weaknesses and struggles. I initially assumed the struggles in her marriage were typical, ordinary, commonplace...I mean, every couple has conflict and challenges. Every woman feels neglected at times or misunderstood.

My assumption was very wrong. I soon became a companion on a journey of pain that began many years before we ever met, and would only grow more traumatic as the days went by.

As I walked beside Joy through the darkness, I saw a woman assert her confidence in God instead of placing it in a man. She showed that claims mean nothing when they are not backed up by choices. I witnessed her surrender her image, but maintain her integrity. I stood in awe (and sometimes anger) as she reacted with quiet grace and patient endurance to every rejection and setback. I watched her refuse to give in to despair.

When well-meaning people insisted that she deny or pretend and call it faith, she held with every last ounce of strength to a God who exposes lies and could handle the truth.

And I learned that hope is not mindlessly believing things will end the way you had in mind. Rather, it is fixing your eyes on the One who endured the Cross—the greatest crisis the world has ever known.

I believe we are guilty, especially at church, of talking about crisis/suffering like it is static. Like, "it may happen," or "what to do when it happens." Like pain is simple and short-lived. Like there are easy answers and guaranteed prescriptions. And even like crises can be avoided if we do the right things and try hard enough.

The truth is, crisis is not straightforward. Sometimes it is chronic. Rather than being predictable, suffering is mysterious and inexplicable. And usually, in spite of our best efforts, or maybe even because of them, it is inevitable.

The testimony I saw firsthand is outlined here for you. My treasured friend has taught me so much. As you confront your crisis, she will hold your hand and walk with you. It may seem that you are facing an all-consuming darkness. I truly believe *Identity Crisis* will be a light to illuminate your path.

This book is for those moments when your life is nothing you thought it would be and everything you hoped it would not. For the times when mere platitudes will not suffice. For those mornings when it is an accomplishment just to get out of bed.

You will not find platitudes here. You will not find unrealistic instructions and empty cliches.

But you will find Hope.

Kristy Andrews

Preface

Sitting at my dining room table, I was emotionally exhausted. I watched the clock with dread. In a matter of minutes I would have to leave my house and drive across town to the lawyer's office. In those moments thirty-two months of pain surfaced. I wrote Psalms 138:7–8 on a note card and tucked it in my purse. The end had come. The deep sense of loss was overwhelming, and fear gripped me.

May 2009, my world fell apart. I was forced to become a student of many things that were beyond my comprehension. Hearing the hurtful words and knowing that the person saying them was hurling them towards my unprotected heart was too much most of the time. I would numb myself with busyness. I would lie in my closet and cry. I would sit in the hardware store's parking lot just to get away from the pain. The pain always accompanied me.

Sitting in a counselor's office and hearing her tell us that what was needed was beyond her expertise made me feel hopeless. Loving someone and watching him refuse to get the help he needed left me feeling completely helpless. Experiencing abandonment was one of my darkest times. Feeling unsafe reinforced fears that paralyze.

My perspective changed when I heard Pastor Johnny Hunt say, "Sometimes God chooses to dig the well of joy with the spade of sorrow." I began to desire a beautiful well of joy to be in the center of the mess that engulfed my life. I desired God to dig a well with his grace, his wisdom, his love, and his purpose. It seems like it was only yesterday that my world turned upside down. Then on other days it feels so long ago. I don't know why you have picked up this book. Maybe you find yourself standing in the ruins left by a terrible crisis. Perhaps you are the person who is continually speaking encouragement to a dear friend devastated by a crisis.

Whatever your reason, I will walk with you and show you the unbreakable promises of the all-wise God who is righteous and kind. His love is more powerful than any blow of a crisis. His grace will grip you when you do not have the strength to hold on. His mercy will cover you when your heart is exposed to deep hurt and excruciating pain.

The Old Testament servant, Nehemiah, made himself available to the hard work of rebuilding. What he accomplished in a short time is amazing. The same God who gave Nehemiah the strength, the discernment, and the motivation to rebuild what others had deemed a disgrace is the same God who will give you all you need. Are you ready to make yourself available to the Lord to rebuild in his time , his way, and with his joy? Nehemiah's account of building the walls and hanging the gates of Jerusalem gives insight that applies to your heart. I hope you will do what Nehemiah and the people of Jerusalem did. "'Let us rise and build.' Then they strengthened their hands to this good work"(Neh. 2:18b, ESV).

My children and I have risen up and chosen to rebuild. Our hands are strong for this good work. We are experiencing the joy of the Lord! The "spade of sorrow" has dug deep in my life and the lives of my children. The pain is intense! I would never desire for anyone to experience the pain of life-altering crisis. However, at some point in life we all are touched by crisis either directly or indirectly. It is my prayer that when a crisis enters your life that you will trust that the spade being used is an opportunity for joy. Surrender to the One who redeems what is ruined, finds what is lost, and gives you his identity.

One of the most difficult things you will face during your crisis may be the lack of desire to worship. It is imperative that you continue to worship, knowing that restoration begins there. Walking in obedience to the Lord will bring continuous clarity to your circumstances. You may not always understand the process by which the Lord uses to bring healing, but you can trust that he knows the process that your heart needs for the healing. The darkness that moves in and seems to place your heart in the dark shadows of uncertainty can cause you to feel afraid. I hope you experience the all-knowing God who sees you. Immersing yourself in the truths of God's Word will be your compass when it is difficult to know what your next step is. When others evaluate your pain and it is too much and causes more pain, you can rest in the arms of the One who knows your heart and will hide you under the shadow of his wings. The Lord will bring you from crisis to credibility in his timing and his way. When he moves you through he will present your life as a beautiful testimony that will draw others to the loving Savior.

I have not written this book as an expert. I have written this book as someone who has lived in a crisis that could not be easily explained or understood, and brought more confusion than clarity. I have experienced the devastation of divorce with details that are not neatly wrapped. I couldn't fix my situation. I couldn't fix other people. And I found that the simple over-spiritualized answers often offered were inadequate in my circumstances. When I didn't know what else to do, I pursued the One who did and found it wasn't answers I needed. It was the Answer. No formula could solve the real complicated issues of my life. My crisis was not alleviated and the mess was still overwhelming. However, my identity was and always will be in the One who brings unspeakable joy to unspeakable pain.

Acknowledgements

I have benefited over the last three years from the strong biblical teachings of Pastor Johnny Hunt. His boldness and faithfulness in preaching Scripture guided me to the light of God's truths during the darkest time I have ever experienced.

I would like to thank Terry Whalin for believing in what I had to offer. The first manuscript had humble beginnings and with deep gratitude I am thankful that he could see the message I desired to convey.

Thank you, Kate Sabott for your invaluable help and many hours of correcting and bringing out my writing style as you edited this book.

Lisa Mount's wise counsel and tender instruction gave me a safe place to begin a healing process that still continues. The hours counseling with my children are a gift and the result of your time continues in their hearts.

I am deeply grateful to Billy Andrews, who walked me and my children through my crisis as a loving pastor and with brotherly love. I am continuously overwhelmed by the love that is daily poured out on us through our pastor and his wife, Brody and Little Holloway. You will never know this side of heaven how great is the impact of your investment on our messy lives. You have never one time been intimidated by our mess! However, you both are intentional to helping us rebuild.

Finally, thanks to all I haven't named but who have put your hands to the good work of rebuilding alongside me and my children

CHAPTER ONE

As I Am

A Mess in Need of Mercy

God allows the pain that throws me into the path of his glory so that I might experience his sovereignty, love, and unlimited grace. I don't know what pain has been allowed into your life. I don't know what crisis has left you shaken. You may be asking, "Now what?" What is the next step that needs to be taken so the pieces are put together? Maybe your crisis began yesterday, or months or years ago. Whenever it struck, I am sure you are looking for the direction that will provide peace and credibility, since your crisis may have caused you to lose your identity. You can't separate who you are from the crisis that has slammed into your life. This predicament seems to define you. When the landscape of my life was permanently changed I didn't want to hear Romans 8:28: "And we know that for those who love God all things work together for good, for those who are called according to his purpose" (ESV). I didn't want to be told that "all things work together for good." I wanted to know what to pick up, where to take what had survived the storm, and how to rebuild and become credible. What I didn't grasp in those early days was the deeper meaning of this verse. As I studied it, I learned that "causes" and "work together" have identical definitions. They both mean to be a fellow worker, to cooperate—help with and work —together. How can a crisis that has taken place under the watchful eye of the sovereign God work together for good? You may wonder where God was when the crisis began. Did God look away and that's why this happened? You may have wondered the age old question: If God is so good then why do bad things happen?

If there is ever a reason to do the good work of rebuilding, it is found in that word. *Good.* It is everything I longed for that was agreeable, excellent, pleasant, joyful, upright, and honorable. I am sure that as you find yourself in the debris of your own crisis, you long for everything to be good. This word is the box that will hold all the tools you need to rebuild.

The broken one living in a crisis longs for the good, the happy, the honorable. The sovereign God works with us so that when we submit to his way of working, we begin to not only see the good, but experience the good.

An Invitation

Pick up your Box of Good and prepare to discover the purpose for which you have been invited to use the tools of God's truth and the power of his principles. You have not been called in the sense of your name being yelled out for all to hear and possibly cause you brief embarrassment. It is not the type of call as if God had nothing to do and chose to pick on you. The word "called" is a Greek word meaning "invitation." This is not just your average invitation. This is an invitation to a banquet. It is a personal invitation. It has your name beautifully monogrammed on the finest paper and it is written in the crimson blood of the Lamb, sealed with holiness, and delivered through the resurrection of Jesus Christ. All is for his purpose. You are for his purpose. Even my devastating crisis and your heartbreaking crisis are for his purpose.

All of these things are for the setting-forth, which is where we are exposed. In Exodus the Lord gave specific instructions for the tabernacle. One of these: "And you shall set the showbread upon the table before Me always" (Exodus 25:30, NKJV). What does "setting forth" have to do with Romans 8:28? The word "purpose" in this verse translates to "showbread," which was set forth, placed in view. The showbread was to be always exposed before God.

For the broken person, therein lays the pain, the fear, the judgment, and the insecurity that make up a crisis. In the exposing, we have the promise of being hidden in Christ. The Lord is not allowing the crisis in your life to expose you to everyone. That will happen to some degree depending on the crisis. However, this purpose is to keep you always before him. When we are before him at all times, he will provide a beautiful garment of grace that will hide us from those who seek to take advantage of our crisis.

Will you, as I have chosen to do, accept the Box of Good? Will you find security in the invitation and, while perhaps being exposed, trust the only One that can give purpose to your pain?

Sometimes the crisis in your life can be the perfect place for others to think they have the liberty to make judgments, give opinions, and assume that not only will your life never be the same, but that it will never be made whole. But while even you may not believe your life will be whole again, dear friend, you are in the perfect place to begin experiencing that his "steadfast love is better than life" (Psalm 63:3, ESV).

Broken Hope

During my own crisis, a time came when I was gripped with fear of never being able to find all the pieces of my broken life. If you can't find the pieces, then how are you to put your life back together? Then I was drawn to the message of hope in the Old Testament book of Nehemiah, which tells the story of a purpose-driven servant who believed that broken things were meant to be rebuilt.

When Nehemiah, a cupbearer to the king, heard the news of his beloved homeland's reproach and disgrace, he wept. Tears and the reality of crisis changing the landscape of your life go hand in hand. Why? Maybe because tears help soften the soil of the soul that finds it difficult to change as quickly as the crisis demands. A crisis seems to demand more from us than we can give. The temptation is to weep and then weep some more. However, there is more meaning to your pain than thousands of teardrops. There is purpose in your pain. Look up and see the One who will shine his glory on your pain. He will have mercy on you. He will provide to make you whole.

As I sought the Lord during those early days of what seemed like bad news delivered before worse news, I was drawn to Nehemiah. The Holy Spirit continued to whisper to my heart and direct me to this book. It intrigued me that Nehemiah responded as he did. For him to receive such horrible news about his homeland and to be in a position where he could do absolutely nothing about it—it seemed hopeless. As a fix-it, Type A, nothing-can-stop-me type person, I was reading this book as if I had discovered an ancestor's journal telling a fantastic story of hope for which I held the key. Hope is the only thing that can give rest from the unpredictability that comes with crisis.

Nehemiah prayed. He did not ask why; in fact, he didn't ask any questions. Instead, he stated what he did know and what he believed. "O LORD God of heaven, the great and awesome God who keeps covenant and steadfast love with those who love him and keep his commandments" (Neh. 1:5, ESV). Has crisis tempted you to falter in your belief in *who* God is? The crisis you experienced has been allowed by the one, true, good God. This is a difficult concept to understand, much less accept. I have often thought that crisis does not come into our lives to give us insight into God, as much as to give us insight into what our life would be like without God. He is too great to understand and he is too vast to comprehend.

But be assured: he still keeps his covenants, and the crisis he has allowed has not changed them or his nature. He also remains steadfastly with those who love him and keep his commandments. His steadfast love is good. He is good.

Pain's Purpose

The pain of crisis can tempt us to become self-centered, perhaps not with arrogance but for the sake of relief. Nehemiah's prayer convicts. One might read his prayer and conclude that crisis is a result of the personal choice to sin. That might be the case for some people, but it is not true for everyone. No matter the "cause" of our crisis, we must keep a right relationship and right perspective of who we are to God. We are sinners. God is holy. Your crisis may not be happening because of outright sin in your life. Many may stand with you and agree that you are blameless. However, your crisis does have your attention. The pain has you in such a position that real relief is found only on your knees.

Nehemiah confessed and admitted not only the sin of his people but his own sin. Surviving a crisis demands we admit that we have fallen short of God's holiness. Then these sweet words uttered by Nehemiah: "They are your servants and your people, whom you have redeemed by your great power and by your strong hand" (Neh. 1:10, ESV). Dear friend, your crisis does not define you. You are redeemed! It is Christ's death on the cross that made the way for our souls to be redeemed from the bondage of sin. In other words, Jesus Christ paid the price for you so that sin may no longer have power over you. If God can save our soul from sin, dear friend, stand firm knowing that the same powerful God will bring you through the crisis. You are in the grip of his strong hand and that is a grip that never gives way or tires of holding you.

Mercy

If pain of the crisis is what brings us to our breaking point, then mercy is what brings hope and small doses of strength to push us through the pain. Nehemiah had to experience mercy from others. When others give us mercy during our time of crisis, they give a great gift. One person's act of mercy can make the way for others to follow suit. Nehemiah knew that the king whom he served may not adjust well to the sadness that Nehemiah could not hide. One of the expectations and requirements was that the cupbearer could never be sad in the king's presence. This made me think of the times when our dearest friends and closest family members have an unrealistic expectation for our emotions.

Sitting in the warm sunshine with my grandmother one day, I finally had the courage to tell her how the landscape of my life was changing and how my crisis was overwhelming me. I did not need courage because she would have chastised me or shamed me. I needed courage because it was so difficult to put words to my pain.

She listened intently and when I had finished, I saw tears running down her face. The tears also welled up in my eyes and then she held me ever so tightly and told me that it was all right for me to cry. Knowing that she had no expectations of me to dismiss my pain or suppress my sadness was freeing.

We should also be careful that we haven't placed unrealistic expectations on ourselves emotionally. A crisis changes us. A crisis affects our countenance. A crisis does not hide; instead, it overshadows and overpowers. The vulnerability that a crisis creates is uncomfortable not only to us but potentially to others. In Nehemiah's case, it was a great risk to be sad in the presence of the king. Nehemiah could not put on a mask and pretend all was well with his soul. To deny your deep pain during your crisis only to make others comfortable is a lure of Satan to tempt you to deal with your pain in ways that will hinder the grace God wants to extend. Others might be uncomfortable with your pain and a few may walk away from you in your time of greatest need. However, your dependence is best set on God and his provisions, not others' reactions. When you place yourself in the hands of the almighty God at the time of your crisis, you also submit to his way of carrying you through the crisis. You begin to live life of the simplest trust.

The simple trust is childlike. You begin to trust that the Lord will get you through the next hour, and then your realize he brought you through twenty-four hours. You trust he will provide physical rest, and you wake the following morning aware of the sleep you were given. You trust he will give answers, and you are given truth from his Word that brings peace you cannot explain. You begin to realize that the simplicity of God's Word provides deep truth that grounds you. You are not tossed about in the strong winds that blow through your crisis. You discover you are experiencing a personal God who cares about every detail of your daily life.

Nehemiah went to work one particular day on which he could not hide his heartbreak or cover up his deep grief. He could not pretend that he was all right. What he needed was mercy. The very person who could decide how Nehemiah's sadness should be dealt with took notice of Nehemiah's countenance. The effects of a crisis can be seen in almost every area of life. Sometimes it is withdrawal from others or activities. Some will deal with their crisis by becoming extremely busy and over-committed. Others may choose to depend on medicine to numb the pain. A few will choose to cope with unhealthy reliance on alcohol, drugs, or relationships. The temptation to cover and guard from others' judgments and opinions is to pretend that all is well. However, at times the heart overwhelms the countenance and the way we live; we cannot hide or pretend. We find ourselves standing completely exposed and our prayer, "Lord, grant me mercy."

Nehemiah ends the first chapter with his identity. "Now I was cupbearer to the king" (Neh. 1:11, ESV). Crisis has a way of making us state what we do, how others identify us, and how we describe ourselves. I don't know how you would finish the statement, "Now I was…" I finished mine with, "Now I was a counselor to the hurting, confused, and depressed." Reading Nehemiah's statement, I wondered if he craved reassurance, felt it necessary to remind himself of who he was, needed to focus on the task before him because keeping it together was all-consuming. Maybe you finish your statement with one of these: pastor's wife, schoolteacher, women's ministry leader, good wife, loving mom, pastor, husband, elder in the church, financially successful, family man. Whatever words you use to sum up who you were to others, a crisis can rip away in cruel fashion. It's like trying to wear clothes you have outgrown; they no longer fit. The only thing that seems to fit comfortably is the realization that you are a mess—no longer put together, completely unglued. You can say "I was a…" all you want, but now you realize that trying to grasp who you are now is like putting a puzzle together with no picture to guide. Overwhelming. Impossible. Wearisome. You completely understand Nehemiah's request for mercy.

Sweet mercy! Lamentations 3:22–23 reminds us, "Through the LORD's mercies we are not consumed, because his compassions fail not. They are new every morning; great is Your faithfulness" (NKJV). When standing in the middle of your crisis that has ruined life as you knew it and stolen your rest and changed everything, because of the Lord's mercy you are *not* consumed. This crisis is not "the end." This crisis will not destroy you. God's mercy is greater than your crisis. The details of your crisis hit hard. Details of this magnitude pull us downward and we can lose perspective. However, the Lord's mercy will never let you be destroyed and will never weaken under the intense blows of any crisis.

Labeled and No Good

My first vivid memory of broken things is from when I was four years old. I was taking a casserole dish back to our neighbor. She had been so kind and brought dinner over when my younger brother was born. The last words my father said to me as I scooted out the door were, "Don't drop it." I made it across the yard and as I turned around her car, I heard a loud crash. There at my feet was the casserole dish in a billion pieces. A billion pieces is an exaggeration. However, to a four-year-old child it might as well have been a billion pieces! So I did what any problem-solving child would do. I ran home, crying, and hid under my bed. My father somehow convinced me not only to come out from underneath my hiding place but to also go with him to tell the neighbor about her broken dish. I have no memory of the exact conversation but I do remember her chatting calmly with my dad and sweeping up the glass.

Where are you hiding? What do you hide behind? Why are you afraid? I have known *about* a certain woman for most of my life. Recently, I have wondered what it would be like to have known her personally. Part of me can relate to a piece of her life story. Specifically, this woman's sense of separation and belief that everyone else's crisis was more important than her own. Jesus' disciples Matthew, Mark, and Luke introduce us to this woman. We do not know her name but we are told about her problem. Her problem was chronic. Her problem left her feeling hopeless and isolated. Luke introduces her this way, "And a woman having an issue of blood twelve years, who had spent all her living upon physicians, and could not be healed of any" (Luke 8:43, ESV). We find this woman's story tucked quietly inside this passage of Scripture where Jesus had calmed a raging storm that terrified his disciples, cast out demons that had tormented a man for years, and was heading to the house of Jarius, whose daughter was dying. While this woman may have broken all protocol that day and joined the crowd, she was desperate. She may have come thinking Jesus was her last hope. I wonder at what point she knew He was her only hope.

Have you thought that your crisis was not as important or as dramatic as others'? I have thought about this woman through the years and wondered if she almost talked herself out of going to see Jesus. I don't know what gave her the courage she needed that day to make her way through the crowds of people. Had she heard that he had calmed the raging storm? Had she overheard others talking about the demon-possessed man who was now in his right mind? As she made her way through the crowd did she overhear Jarius' plea for Jesus to come very quickly to his house and heal his dying daughter? Was she afraid that someone would realize she was amongst the crowd and make her leave at once? Perhaps she had family and friends who encouraged her to go see

Jesus because, if he could heal the sick, then just maybe he might be able to heal her.

Her crisis labeled her unclean. That is what a crisis does: it labels. Divorce is my label. Maybe drug abuser is your label. The alcoholic label you wish you could rid yourself of remains because others have a hard time letting it go. Maybe you think that others see your silent label of the child abuse you suffered and you live with shame. You may be desperately wanting to tell the truth behind your label of anger and depression but are fearful of others knowing about the abortion you had. Too many labels to list and too much pain carried by the individuals who wear them...but all desire to be made whole.

This woman's label was a problem not only for her, but also for others. If she touched anyone else, that person was made unclean for an amount of time. For her to make her way through a crowd was not easy or accepted. Furthermore, this woman was broke. Luke tells us that she had spent all she had on doctors. No one could help her. A crisis will have you looking for help at any cost. A crisis will label your life whether you want it to or not. On this particular day the woman had Nehemiah's brand of courage when he risked his life going before the king with a sad countenance. This woman went to Jesus, risking condemnation from those she might contaminate.

Maybe she thought she could make her way through the crowd unseen and quietly leave after touching the hem of his garment. Everything she thought could happen did not happen and everything she hoped to happen did happen. I wonder if she ever thought that she would have Jesus' undivided attention. Yet that is exactly what had to happen! No one can enter into the presence of the King of Kings and be made whole without having his undivided attention.

The moment she touched the hem of his garment, Jesus knew. He could have continued on his way and never publically acknowledged this woman. The divine healing could have only been known between the two of them and then maybe a doctor would have confirmed that she had been healed. But when you are made whole through the power of the Almighty God, people know. It cannot be hidden, it cannot be kept quiet, and it cannot go unnoticed. Even though Jarius was depending on Jesus to be quick in getting to his house and healing Jarius' daughter—and even though nothing would stop Jesus from getting to a little girl who needed him—he still had all the time in the world to stop and give his undivided attention to a woman who had been unseen, who may by this point in her life have felt forgotten and unimportant. Don't ever think that your crisis is less important or less traumatic. It isn't your crisis that has God's attention. *You* have his attention.

A crisis changes so much. For Nehemiah it changed his priorities. He wasn't all that concerned with what the king would think or how he would react. He only knew that he needed to go to Jerusalem and follow the Lord's direction. He had to leave the presence of an earthly king and be present for the use of the eternal King.

For this woman in Luke 8, crisis had changed her perspective. For years she had been forced to live confined. She did not have the same freedoms as others. Had she given up? After all, no physician could help her. While a crisis has a way of changing our perspective, like this woman it was the hope of healing that gave her purpose.

Hope will give purpose. I don't know everything this woman felt that day as she made her way to Jesus. I don't know what your day or your past days have looked like as you make your way through the rubble your crisis has left behind. I know for me there came *that day* when nothing else mattered but the promise of healing—the promise of being whole—and that gave me purpose to make my way to the One who could deliver on his promise. I was not concerned with what others said. I was not concerned with what others thought. I did not let anything get in my way. On *that day* everything I did was on purpose, to get to the One who gave me purpose and brought purpose to my pain.

So here you are a mess, a mess in need of mercy. Before you and I can begin to rebuild, we must seek purpose in the pain. Live on purpose for the One who gives purpose. We must understand why our life and all that encompasses living can be redeemed. Paul said it best when he wrote to Timothy, "The saying is trustworthy and deserving of full acceptance, that Christ Jesus came into the world to save sinners, of whom I am the foremost. But I received mercy for this reason, that in me, as the foremost, Jesus Christ might display his perfect patience as an example to those who were to believe in him for eternal life. To the King of the ages, immortal, invisible, the only God, be honor and glory forever and ever. Amen" (1 Timothy 1:15–17, ESV). I would do more harm to your hurting heart if I only acknowledged the pain that accompanies a crisis. If there is not a deeper understanding of the One who will heal, then all the words are written in vain.

Just as Nehemiah understood at the moment when his heart broke and he heard the devastating news, the only way through the devastation has to be done with humility before the almighty God. You and I must come to understand that Jesus Christ came for one reason: to save sinners. It is this reason and this reason alone that we have found mercy. We are the examples to others of a patient, sovereign God.

As you stand in the midst of the crisis that has changed everything, remember this has passed through his hands first. God is in control. He sustains you. He is the lifter of your head. He redeems. He provides. He makes beauty from ashes. He sees you. He is your light in the darkness. He has a plan to restore your life. You will feel the pain of your life falling apart. Others are watching your life change to something that will never be quite the same as it was before. Will you do the hard work and the heart work that lies ahead, committing to do all things for the glory of the Lord? Will you trust that the details of rebuilding are God's defining moments for you? Will you entrust yourself to the process the Lord has for you believing in the end your life will not be about the crisis, but a life redeemed?

CHAPTER TWO

Unexpected

Do What You Need to Do

Emotions triggered by a crisis can be completely overwhelming. The more you fight the emotions, the worse you feel. You fear that if you completely give into the strong current, the emotions will take you under and you may never break the surface into a joy-filled life. In the early days, weeks, and months of my crisis, I found myself between great sadness, fear of being vulnerable to others seeing my pain, and fear of being judged. Maybe part of the reason the pain of crisis is so deep is that so much of the pain is private. As a counselor, I saw the deep, intense pain that others brought to me in confidence. It was the part of the story they had never told that increased the intensity of the pain. Is it private because it is never spoken about? Does this pain remain silent because there are no words to describe?

Whatever your reason for not saying what you are feeling and how deeply you hurt, I hope you will experience that unexpected moment when someone takes notice of your pain. Whether they take notice on their own accord or they take notice because you reach out does not change the impact of that unexpected moment. One of the many reasons I kept returning to the powerful story of a simple man and his relentless pursuit to rebuild a city was that I saw myself in his story.

Unexpected Attention

Even though he was grief-stricken, Nehemiah did what he needed to do by going to work and performing his job (Neh. 2:1-6). Just like you, I also get up every morning and do what I need to do for the day. Grief does not stop the clock. Devastating news does not put the world on pause. A life-changing crisis will not allow you to rewind time. Each day comes and each day ends. You learn to greet each sunrise doing your best to work your way through the hours. You end the day knowing you made it through. This sounds discouraging. It sounds dreadful. It is.

Then Nehemiah had his unexpected moment! The king noticed Nehemiah's sadness and Nehemiah was afraid. Fear heaped on top of great grief can cause you to buckle underneath the weight. The heart can only handle so much. I wonder if Nehemiah had thought through this scenario. I have stood with grieving mothers who have buried their child. I cringe when I hear her being asked, "How are you doing?" I think to myself, *They would not be able to handle the answer if she were really honest with the answer.* It is the mystery of living in crisis mode. Do you answer the question, "What's wrong?" How much do you say? Your pain pleads with your heart to let it all out, but you fear what the reaction will be. You stand in the balance between fear and hope. The choices are: total exposure and the risk of harsh judgment, or making light of "just a bad day" and living a lie. Agony.

How do you respond in that moment when you stand at the mercy of the person who could make it better or worse and you hear as Nehemiah did, "What are you requesting?" In other words, "What do you need?" When your life has been devastated by a crisis, you only have needs. You forget desires, wants, and wishes. You just want the basic necessities: understanding, a listening ear, love, support, and acceptance. Suddenly the perks of your life before the crisis are trivial. You don't need a lot of "friends." You need a few who will walk through the crisis with you—the kind who are strong and grounded and not intimidated by your pain. You need the kind of people in your life that can walk in the dark because deep, abiding faith in Christ is the only compass they use. Those are the people who can help lead you. Those are the people who will help guard you. Those are the people the Lord will use to hold you up.

When you are in the midst of a crisis, superficial relationships are cut loose with ease. You don't need people who are in your life because they only want the details of how all of this happened. In the early months of experiencing heart wrenching sadness, I was deeply wounded when I shared lunch with someone I considered a friend. She sought information about my situation and then she took the information she had with no attempt to understand, then made severe judgments. This experience added stress to my already weary and emotional heart. I did not want to talk to just anyone about my circumstances. Others can and will present concern and care for your circumstances, but what you need is people in your life who will help you make the next step toward restoration and wholeness. I had five individuals plus a wonderful Christian counselor who helped show me the next steps. For you, it may be more or it may be fewer who play this role. It isn't the number that matters; it is about who is capable to guide you with godly counsel and wisdom.

Knowing what you need can be difficult. When a crisis has left you in darkness and destruction, you have to let yourself feel the weight of it and then refocus to begin to see your life after the crisis. What is that going to look like? What can be salvaged? What has to change? What do I need to begin the rebuilding process? Who will help me?

The Unknown

The unknown can cause you to be more fearful. Trying to imagine your life after the crisis has hit is almost impossible. For many of us, we never expected the crisis. Maybe this describes you, too. One day your life was as normal as ever and then suddenly everything you have known changes and you feel completely misplaced. You have been forced to enter into a life you do not know and cannot begin to comprehend. You find yourself staring in the mirror and you realize you don't totally recognize the person staring back. The deep sadness in your eyes. The tired, worn-out complexion. The downward curve of your mouth. This person bears little resemblance to the person who at one time had bright eyes, a warm complexion, and a contagious smile.

I wish I could tell you exactly what your life will be like now that the harsh blows of your crisis have hit and destroyed. The mystery of a crisis is that it is different for each of us. Maybe a more appropriate perspective is to understand that each crisis is specifically designed for the person in the crisis. When we come to that place where we accept and understand that our crisis can be used for a purpose, we can begin to see how the crisis can transform us. God is sovereign over the storm. Colossians 1:16–18 reflects the truth that will bring us into right perspective of who we are in light of an omnipotent God. "For by him all things were created, in heaven and on earth, visible and invisible, whether thrones or dominions or rulers or authorities—all things were created through him and for him. And he is before all things, and in him all things hold together. And he is the head of the body, the church. He is the beginning, the firstborn from the dead, that in everything he might be preeminent" (ESV).

Even though you might be in the most excruciating pain the soul can endure or body can withstand, this truth remains. God is supreme over your crisis. He has authority over your pain. He holds all things, including you and your crisis. The same God who is present in your crisis is already in the future of your crisis. Time cannot constrain the One who created it and rules it.

Does this mean that God creates havoc? No. He is not the author of confusion (1 Corinthians 14:33). I think when we are being consumed by the turmoil and unrest that comes with any crisis we become focused on wanting God to change our circumstance and give us relief. However, the question that needs to be asked is: If nothing changes or gets better, will you continue to trust the sovereignty of the indescribable God? First Peter 2:21 presents this kind of trust: "For to this you have been called, because Christ also suffered for you, leaving you an example, so that you might follow in his steps" (ESV). What are we called to? We are called to suffer with patience and follow the example of Christ.

I want to encourage you as I was once encouraged. Don't be so focused on trying to figure out what your life will be like once the crisis settles, but rather focus on how your heart will be changed and affected. The temptation is to get ahead and try to make your life fit what you're going through. But living each day at a time and seeking wisdom for how your life should reflect God's purpose will give you deeper perspective and a greater trust in him. I spent the beginning months of my own crisis trying to see the other side and picture what my life would be like. I never could see it. If you and I stood on the beach of the Atlantic Ocean, we would never expect to see the other side. Before us would be a vast ocean, and we can only see so far. We would only ever see the other side by traveling there in a boat or plane. What I had to believe in those early months was that if God walked with me to the storm, then he would also be with me through the storm. The only way to the other side was through it. When you make the choice to go through the storm then your life can reflect God's purpose for you in and after the crisis. You will know the Lord in a way that only can be seen during the darkest and scariest times.

The Heart's Need

God will change the heart. I hope that your heart will become more tender, compassionate, loving, sensitive, strong, desirous of God's ways and timing, and eager for what he has planned for you. It is easy—much too easy—for the heart to be affected by a crisis and turn away from God, becoming bitter, angry, stuck, blame-casting, unforgiving, resistant to grace, and demanding of answers. The great challenge in the beginning of your crisis is to worship the One who has all authority while still feeling the weight of the grief and shock of what has changed your life as you know it. Worshipping with a heavy heart can almost seem pointless. We like to enjoy worship with a heart overflowing with joy and gratitude and when it overflows with pain and grief it is a much different experience. Much like when the sun shines at the same time the rain is falling. You find you want both and may need both. When sun and rain come together, you simply wonder how that can be. Worship while in crisis mode is the same. You have both of the things that will change you: the thing has already changed life this side of Heaven, and the thing that will continue to change you for eternity and bring peace during the trials this side of heaven.

The very nature of a crisis demands quick response to what can and cannot be salvaged. You realized quickly that the crisis changes things whether or not you are ready for it. Then there comes a day when you dare ask yourself: "How do I rebuild and who will help me?"

It can be extremely difficult to see your way through the crisis. Like driving in thick fog, all you can do is turn your lights on, grip the steering wheel, and move through it ever so slowly. All the while you hope nothing gets in your way, but you do know that at some point the fog will lift. So many days are like that thick fog. You are weary. You just want to see something that will let you know it is almost over. It doesn't take much to give you the slightest bit of hope and it doesn't take much to leave you feeling defeated. Fragile is the only way to describe your heart.

The Heart's Need

Hope comes when you have a realization as Nehemiah did when the king asked what he needed. I wonder if Nehemiah felt less overwhelmed when he realized that the king not only had noticed his pain but also recognized that he had needs. I hope that you, too, have been given someone who has stepped in and cared for you when he or she did not have to. When I received this kind of compassion from five dear friends, I realized very quickly that these were not just friends, they were treasures! Once I opened up to the first of them, my feelings of being overwhelmed, scared, lonely, unsure, and distressed lessened a bit. One particular woman looked at me with the gentlest eyes; as I watched tears well up in those eyes, she asked me what I needed. I could not answer her. To be honest, I was only aware of my pain and had not thought of what I needed.

Being able to focus on what I needed to rebuild helped me work through the pain.

Living through the beginning of a crisis can seem a blur, but there comes a time when you tire of the blur and are ready for clarity. You have gone through the motions of daily life on autopilot, and you suddenly desire to be moving forward with purpose. So often, we begin to realize what we need, but having what we need requires honesty. This honesty comes by admitting our lack with complete vulnerability. As I read in Nehemiah 2, I respected this man who knew that he had to ask for and what he needed if there was to be any hope for his goal. This humble servant knew he needed to rebuild the city he loved. That was the obvious need. He was able to also know what it would take for him to accomplish complete rebuilding. He would need time. He would need a place for his own shelter. His success in rebuilding would also depend on the authority of the king. Nehemiah needed the king to make way through the threatening areas.

Time is necessary when you are in the restoration process. Nehemiah gave the king a timeframe of his absence and his return. While time cannot be demanded upon when you are healing, I do think it is healthy to not leave life open-ended. Set small goals for yourself. Marking goals can help you be wise with the time of the healing process.

Having others stand with you can bolster the courage needed to face people who seem to be against you or do not take the time to understand your crisis. Nehemiah was also aware of his own needs to take care of himself. Even though he would need timber to be able to rebuild the city, he also needed to make himself a place to take refuge. Above all, Nehemiah understood he could not accomplish what needed to be done without the authority of the king. It is the same with us. We can state our needs and be fully aware of the details of the need, but if we move forward without relying on the authority of Jesus Christ, we will fail. Some will never have what they want because they are too prideful to ask for what they need. I don't know where you are in your crisis. Most likely you do know that you want peace, joy, understanding, rest, a lighter load, and acceptance. Knowing and stating right now where you can find shelter and care might be the very thing you need to move toward these.

Let me explain, this is not a formulaic prosperity message: think positive thoughts and all that is good will automatically come to you. This is about making the difficult choice that puts you in a position to do the hard work. For me, it was going to counseling and seeking truth and answers. I was afraid because I feared what "truth" would be learned. I submitted to a process that was grueling. I listened, even when I didn't want to, to professional counselors, a pastor, and the five women in my life. The majority of the time they were encouraging but there were times when one or two of them would tell me truth that stung. However, I needed to hear it. I needed to process it. I needed to search my heart and know if what had been spoken did apply to me. They each had a perspective I did not have. So not only did I lean on them, I listened to them.

I also submitted to God's authority. He made me. He created my heart. He knew my needs better than I did or still do. I am passionate for you to understand that our motive in asking for what you need should not be to manipulate the process or to find the fastest way to get what we want. Our motive has to be pure. Our motive needs to be for the purpose of restoration and rebuilding. When we begin to manipulate to get what we want, we become selfish and self-absorbed. When we remain committed to the needs that lead to restoration, we become dependent on the Lord and trust him through the process.

Time is what it takes to restore. Be aware of how your wants will tempt you to rush time. The practical daily living while rebuilding takes focus and determination. Don't let your wants rob you of the beautiful provisions that can be experienced in the practical, everyday rebuilding. Your purpose in stating what you need is so that you will live the next weeks, months, and years hoping for and experiencing God's total supply of all your needs. He will give every good and perfect gift from above, and he will direct your steps.

Passing Through

The king gave Nehemiah what he requested, which was the freedom to move forward and rebuild. The cruelty of a crisis is how easy we can get stuck in our personal disaster and not move. "Let me pass through" was Nehemiah's seemingly simple request (Neh. 2:7). That is the heart's cry when a crisis has you stuck. People who have not experienced devastation do not understand. How many mornings did I wash my face thinking only, "I just need to get through today." Nehemiah stood before the king understanding that he needed to have something proving that the king's authority had been granted so that no one would bother Nehemiah as he made his way to his homeland. The king's authority would allow Nehemiah to pass through.

There will always be that person who does not understand what you are doing. Don't let that person discourage you. Dear one, you can stand firmly on the authority of Scripture. In Nehemiah's day, the letter from the king would not only allow Nehemiah to pass through dangerous territory. Nehemiah also needed a shelter and the supplies for rebuilding: "…give me timber to make beams for the gates of the fortress of the temple, and for the wall of the city, and for the house that I shall occupy" (Neh. 2:8, ESV). What he didn't need was to be bothered. It isn't that Nehemiah minded answering questions; he just didn't want to answer everyone's questions. A crisis demands this type of tunnel vision. All he wanted was to pass through. He didn't have time to be stuck! So with the authority of the king he made his way through with confidence. Once you know what you need to begin the process of rebuilding, it is amazing how focused you become. Some may misunderstand the tunnel vision life you now lead. As you begin your way toward the promise of restoration you become more aware of what could distract you. I wonder if Nehemiah knew that passing through certain areas could be more of a distraction than a deterrent. Distractions can slow our progress. I know during a certain time I cut out any activity that did not promote, support, and facilitate my rebuilding. I will admit that it was tough at first. There were no television shows, late night outings with girlfriends, or frivolous spending. However, there was counseling for me and my children, Bible study and journaling, quality time spent with my children, conversation with my accountability partners, and worship and service at my local church. Above all, there was time given for the purpose of knowing God and discovering what he was doing in my heart.

We have the authority of THE KING! Our salvation is the only "letter" we need to pass through a crisis. The power of a personal, saving relationship with God is what enables us to move through. Romans 1:16 encourages us to be bold: "For I am not ashamed of the gospel, for it is the power of God for salvation to everyone who believes, to the Jew first and also to the Greek" (NASB). Like Nehemiah's letter gave him boldness in facing whoever or whatever would try to stop him, the gospel of Jesus Christ gives us boldness—because it is bold. Jesus left heaven, came to earth, lived among men, was tempted in every way and never sinned, spent three years in ministry preaching salvation, healing disease, calming storms, feeding the five thousand, and revealing the hearts of men. He died a cruel death on the cross. Three days later he conquered death and arose. What other power are you looking for? Your salvation is all you need to pass through. God's great love that we will never comprehend this side of heaven is a relentless love that will help you get through. He is calling you to a life restored because only he can redeem. He promises that he will not let anything separate you from his great love (Romans 8:38–39).

Unpack

We don't need to pack for the long part of the journey called Crisis; we need to unpack. As I realized that my unpacking was the most important part of my journey, I understood Philippians 1:6 as never before: "being confident of this very thing, that he who has begun a good work in you will complete it until the day of Jesus Christ" (NKJV). Be content with what you have, for Deuteronomy states that he "will not leave you or forsake you" (Deut. 31:6, ESV). Hebrews 13:6 reminds us that we can "confidently say, 'The Lord is my helper; I will not fear; what can man do to me?'" (ESV).

Unpack for what lies ahead, move through with the Lord's confidence, stand firm on his authority. This takes great humility and complete transparency. You cannot move through the crisis alone, and you must be completely dependent and grace-filled.

Unpack? Yes, the journey through a crisis demands that you unpack opinion, defensiveness, bitterness, resentment, self-reliance, judgment, and pride. Leave it all behind. Leaving it all behind can be easier said than done. This process is different for each person. However, it is necessary for every person. The unpacking process can only be successful when done through praying and seeking wisdom. My time of unpacking began in my counseling sessions. My deep wounds had also developed into an attitude of bitterness and very unhealthy self-reliance. I spent time talking this out with my closest friends. Journaling became a healing agent for me. It is through journaling I can process what I am feeling and how the Lord is meeting my emotional needs. As you pray and seek the Lord with all your heart during this time, it is imperative that you take responsibility for your emotions and how you are being affected. Unloading is dumping things in a careless manner, whereas unpacking is done with care.

The strength you need requires a complete emptying yourself and readying to be filled with God's strength, power, and grace. Life after a crisis will never look like the one you had before the crisis. There may be moments where things seem familiar, but it is never the same. Ask that single mom who not only is the breadwinner of the home but also carries the unseen burden of a broken family and desires healing for wounds that only the heart knows. Ask the parents who have buried a child. Ask the hard working employee who has spent years providing for his family and now wonders how the bills will be paid because there is no more work. Ask the spouse driving into the cemetery to put flowers on the grave of the one who should have lived much longer. The loneliness engulfs the heart and screams with grief over the loss. Ask the family of the addict that once again is in bondage to the drug. Ask the woman who is excited to prepare a nursery and choose that specific name only to hear "I'm sorry" as the doctor cannot find a heartbeat. Life is forever changed.

To have life changed and ripped from you is only the beginning. When you realize the depth of the crisis and choose to be empty of everything unhealthy that you are holding on to, then and only then are you able to pass through. It is that unexpected moment that prepares you to move along the way the Lord has provided. Because you are empty, you can now fully receive.

As I read more about Nehemiah's early days journeying, I found comfort in the choice he made when he stated, "and I told no one what God had put into my heart" (Neh. 2:12, ESV). There are times before the hard work can begin of rebuilding when it is not right to express all that the Lord is showing you and the way he is directing you. Some of the sweetest times of communion with your Heavenly Father will be realized in the unexpected moments. When he speaks into your loneliness so loudly that it startles your soul, you know he is there. He will never abandon you.

On a hot summer day two years ago, I had one of many unexpected moments. I am deeply grateful that the Creator of the Universe gives personal attention to our pain. On this particular day, I was in great anguish. That is the only way I know how to describe the state of my heart. I was distressed, feeling deep sorrow, and my pain made my body ache. After reading Nehemiah 2, I was wishing I could have a letter from a king giving me confidence that I would make it through. Call it a pity party, a jealous tantrum, or whatever you would like. I was getting more desperate. A crisis has that kind of power; it can create desperation, distress, depression, and doubt. I wanted to have confidence. I wanted to feel confident. Instead, I felt unsure.

All I really wanted was for someone to tell me I would be all right. My King answered my heart's cry. The all-powerful and all-wise God gave me what he knew I needed. I was reading a portion of Psalm during my quiet time; whatever my reason was, the Lord had a great purpose. When my eyes read the words "a promise," I wept. When your heart is breaking and gripped by fear of the unknown, you need assurance and perspective as much as you need oxygen for your next breath. Psalm 138:8 is a powerful prayer: "The Lord will accomplish what concerns me; your loving kindness, O Lord, is everlasting; Do not forsake the works of Your hands" (NASB). Just as I needed to know, you need to know (*really* know) that Jehovah will accomplish what concerns you.

A crisis introduces new concerns all the time. Things you never thought about before may now consume your thoughts. Yet, the Lord will accomplish these concerns. He will not forsake you. This gave me a confidence I had not experienced since the devastation of my own crisis began. When you have the confidence of the Lord in the midst of great trials and deep pain, you have exactly what you need to begin to move forward with purpose. A confident heart is more than words can express, but a heart confident in the Lord is more than the world can explain.

CHAPTER THREE

Landscape
of the Heart

Say Nothing at All

You may be reading this and your crisis has been public to everyone since the beginning. You could be like me and very few knew of your crisis—in fact, many are still unaware. You could be wondering when the moment will come when someone finds out about your crisis and what that will be like. The day my world changed, I sat, I cried, I cleaned, I sat, I cried, I went to the grocery store, and I wondered where to turn. I remember thinking at least if someone had died my house would be full of people offering help and love and support, and someone would have brought a potato salad. But it was just me, alone with my thoughts and my broken heart and my house absent of people and potato salad. My house was instead filled with quiet tears hidden from the giggles of my children, a lot of unanswered questions, and fear of what was to come next. The next morning came as would every morning over the next thirty-six months.

Everything had changed. I, like others, needed the rugged, raw strength of the Savior. You don't want sweet syrupy words of sympathetic prayers. You need the firm command of the Creator telling you to stand up, get a grip (in him), lift up your eyes... your Redeemer has come (Luke 21:28). Then you need to shut your mouth, be still, and look at yourself in the midst of the devastation.

It is not pretty! I am deeply grateful for the women God placed in my life at the onset of my crisis who would call it what is was: a complete mess. They never once sugarcoated anything to make me or themselves feel more comfortable. It is impossible to be comfortable when your life has been blown up by a crisis. The crucial thing is to get over yourself, look at the mess and call it what it is—and then be quiet.

A Quiet Heart

Of course, being quiet is the most difficult thing to put into action when your world has fallen apart. Maybe this is why we read in the last chapter that Nehemiah took a ride in the dark to see the damage of Jerusalem. Nehemiah arrived in Jerusalem and I imagine he was flooded with many different emotions. He had arrived safely and with no problem because of the letter from the king (Nehemiah 2:9). He had also had his first hint that not everyone was particularly thrilled that the people of Jerusalem were being cared for. In light of his journey, a time of quiet was compelling. Maybe he needed to be quiet because he could not separate himself from the damage. Maybe he realized he didn't need (at least in the beginning) people talking to him all at once. In Nehemiah 2 he was with a few men and knew what he was supposed to do. The first few hours, days and weeks into your crisis are so significant. It is imperative that you have the quiet times, the time to take in the damage, the time to cry when no one else sees our tears, the time to begin to have some hope and see the possibility of a life restored. It is not time that will heal your wounds. However, you need time.

You need to have time alone. You need to allow yourself to feel the weight of all that you have lost and experienced. So many times we like having busy schedules, noise, entertainment, chattering people, and any kind of distraction that will guarantee we are never left alone with our thoughts. If you are already giving into that tempting offer then you are robbing yourself of perspective and seeds of hope that can be planted during the times of loneliness and grief. Communion with El Roi, the God Who Sees (Gen. 16:13), will give you strength to rebuild. Make time for the quiet reflection and the quiet realization that all is different but not all is lost. Emerge out of those quiet times with a deeper gratitude to the One who will direct your steps.

You do not have to tell everyone everything. You do not owe everyone an explanation. You do not have to give all the details of how your crisis has changed your life. Simply choose to be aware of what all has been devastated and while knowing, be quiet. After all, neither you nor I want to leave a legacy that begins with "Then it happened" and ends with "She or he never got over it."

My prayer is to encourage you to do something with the crisis that God has allowed to enter your life. Take it all in. Stop hiding behind covered eyes. Look at the damage and call it by name. Maybe it is death, cancer, miscarriage, a stillborn child, chronic illness, addiction, divorce, or financial ruin; whatever it is, don't run from it. Face it.

Nehemiah took a ride in the dark and realized that the descriptions "distress" and "reproach" was the only name fit for the damage he saw (Neh. 1:3, 2:17). That may have been what he called the city's condition but it was not the people's identity. Whatever name fits your crisis, it is a name only. The crisis does not define you! The ability to name something by calling the crisis what it truly is gives you the sense of knowing where you are. Nehemiah knew he was at the place of Distress and Reproach. He also knew he wanted to arrive at Restored and Renewed. Maybe your place is "grief and loneliness" or "sad and confused" or "shock and fear" or "tried and failed" or "hopeless and weary." Whatever your crisis is, there's a name that describes it perfectly.

A Confident Heart

With confidence Nehemiah was able to call the devastation of Jerusalem as it was and he asked for help because rebuilding can never be done alone. The purpose for rebuilding your life after a crisis is to no longer be a reproach, but to live a post-crisis life that does not reek of smoldering shame and disgrace. Instead, we are called by the King to begin the hard work of rebuilding. It will be the most difficult thing you have ever done up to this point. The emotional stamina needed will seem impossible. Continuously renewing of the mind through the truth of God's Word is necessary for the task at hand. While walking through the rubble of your crisis, you will need truth and grace to give you balance.

Truth

Truth gives security. Grace gives safety. How can truth give security when it seems that knowing truth is what gives a crisis its over-powering strength to devastate? Truth, regardless of how it hurts, is the only thing that will give those first glimmerings, thoughts, and experiences of hope. If we only accept truth that gives us good feelings and a positive outlook, then we become out of balance.

By doing so we also have redefined truth by how we want it to affect us. Several years ago I was terrified upon learning of a medical condition: cancer. However, it was the truth of my condition that led to good health. Had I not been told or had not accepted its reality then the cancer would have led to my death. Truth and what you do with that truth can lead to your life filled with peace, joy, hope, and strength.

- Psalm 25:5: "Lead me in your truth and teach me, for you are the God of my salvation; for you I wait all the day long" (ESV).
- Psalm 40:11: "You, O LORD, will not withhold your compassion from me; Your lovingkindness and Your truth will preserve me" (NASB).
- Psalm 51:6: "Behold, You desire truth in the innermost being, and in the hidden part you will make me know wisdom" (NASB).
- John 1:17: "For the Law was given through Moses; grace and truth were realized through Jesus Christ" (NASB).
- John 14:6: "Jesus said to him, 'I am the way, the truth, and the life; no one comes to the Father but through Me'" (NASB).

We have to have truth like we have to have oxygen. Truth will lead you. Truth will preserve you. Truth must settle deep within your soul. Moses was used to give the law—the what to do and what not to do; Jesus gives the "how to" through a relationship with him. You may not know at this very moment what needs to be done to begin to rebuild. If you will commit to be completely dependent on Jesus, accepting that he is the truth, the way, and the life then even in your mess you are right where you need to be.

Nehemiah had to take a good look at the damage. He had to know exactly what the problems were. He had to see it for himself. By realizing how great the damage was and accepting that the task at hand was greater than what he could do himself, he had the right perspective of his total dependence on God. I wonder if Nehemiah had a deeper understanding of how insignificant, helpless, and useless he was and would be if he did not acknowledge that only God and God alone could rebuild the ruins and supply the strength to accomplish the task.

Grace

Why is it so important to name the crisis, calling it what it truly is? The moment you give it a name you are ready to receive the grace that will carry you through. Grace. We say it is amazing. We describe it as unlimited. Can we really comprehend what it does? The Greek word is "charis," meaning that which affords joy, pleasure, delight. It is merciful kindness by which God, exerting his holy influence upon souls, turns them to Christ and keeps, strengthens, and increases them in faith. I wonder as Nehemiah made his way back to the place where he would sleep if he truly understood the grace that would be needed to sustain him.

Dear one, I wish I could sit with you and hear your story about the day the crisis changed the landscape of your life. I am sure there would be a lot of tears, shared and understood silence, and tender smiles. I would listen to you and I would encourage you with the grace of Jesus Christ. He sustains you. He will strengthen you. He will grip you with a holy strength. In his grace you are safe.

You can sit quietly for now and look at the damage done by an unexpected crisis. You can choose to say nothing for the time being. You are looking at life with few answers and many questions. Quietly experience the truth of the crisis knowing that the mighty

God, the everlasting Father, the Prince of Peace, and Wonderful Counselor will bring truth to your crisis. As you strain to see all that has been ruined, fall deep into his grace completely trusting that in his grace you have found the safest place.

CHAPTER FOUR

Where to Begin

The Heart's Desire

True worship demands the sacrificial offering of yourself; more specifically, the innermost part of your soul. It is that act of worship that is holy and acceptable to God. He is not concerned with the mechanics of your worship as much as he is concerned with what you bring to the time of worship—yourself. He may or may not change the details of your crisis. However, he can and will change you.

It is making the time and taking the time to worship. Being aware of all the areas of your life that need to be laid on the altar to be sacrificed before the Lord. You being that "living sacrifice, holy and acceptable, to God which is your spiritual worship" (Romans 12:1, ESV). In other words, as you worship in the midst of your crisis, you are also dying to your wants. You sacrifice yourself so that you can live freely in Christ. Worship is not a feeling that is warm and fuzzy nor is it only emotional. Worship will demand something. Twenty years ago, I heard the author Max Lucado speak. I do not remember anything he said except this one sentence. His statement was so powerful that it has remained with me all these years. He said, "The greatest form of worship is our obedience." To live a life in obedience to the Lord should never be lived only in the comfortable times. When we choose to walk in obedience, it will mean doing so in our most difficult times.

To live one's life as a living sacrifice gives the mental images of death. I did not treasure having to think this way because when life is lived in crisis mode, so many things die. Dreams die in a crisis. Future hopes die. For some, it has been a person dearly loved who has died. For me, my marriage died. I am sure you could add many more to this small list. What does this mean? You may be thinking, *Haven't I already suffered enough!* If there is one thing I hope I can convey to you is that this type of sacrifice is the only type of sacrifice that will promise life.

For me to begin to experience the healing that I desperately desired and continue to need, I had to sacrifice all of it: my expectations, my dreams, my hopes, my ideals, my bitterness, my anger, my loneliness, my demands, my grief, my failure, my self-pity, my thoughts, and my ways.

The Temptation to Present Well

The most tempting part of putting your life back together after a crisis may be the urge to make everything look outwardly presentable. After all, we have a tendency to think that if the outside is presentable, then maybe we really are alright. This temptation is so appealing that God addresses it in the Old Testament. When the prophet Samuel was given the task to find a king to rule over Israel after the Lord had rejected Saul as king, Samuel was given clear instructions about where to find the next king. He was also given a standard for how the Lord sees individuals. "For the LORD sees not as man sees: man looks on the outward appearance, but the Lord looks on the heart" (1 Samuel 16:7b, ESV). The heart issue is frequently addressed throughout the New Testament. Hebrews 4:12 states, "For the word of God is living and active, sharper than any two-edged sword, piercing to the division of soul and of spirit, of joints and of marrow, and discerning the thoughts and intentions of the heart" (ESV). When everything is stripped away the one thing that matters most—because it is the only thing that matters—is our heart.

The dilemma that comes with living in the devastation of a crisis is to convince ourselves and others that if we can appear "normal" then others will be more comfortable with our circumstances. I want to tell you, I don't have it all together. I only hope that as I share the truths found in God's Word you will be encouraged and find strength in him to get up, be gripped by his grace, and rebuild. Don't worry about having it all together. Some people prefer all their ducks to be in a row. To be honest, it will be a good day if all my ducks show up at the pond. Our lives coming back together after a crisis is not for the purpose of making others comfortable. It is only to be a testimony to God's grace and his way of restoration. Some people may struggle with that, because your life will not be what they prefer. However, a life built on preference is shallow at best. A life built in Christ will be unshakeable.

Worship

As I read Nehemiah, I was intrigued by where they began to rebuild. The first gate mentioned in Nehemiah is the Sheep Gate. "Then

Eliashib the high priest rose up with his brothers the priests, and they built the Sheep Gate. They consecrated it and set its doors" (Neh. 3:1, ESV). It is believed that the priests consecrated the Sheep Gate because it led to the temple; here, the rebuilding began and where they committed the city and its walls to God's divine protection. Similarly, our rebuilding after a crisis begins with the sanctification of our heart. In other words, we are to dedicate our lifestyle to God and to be set apart, doing even—as Matthew Henry emphasized—our "common actions *after a godly sort*"[1]. Rebuilding and restoration begins through worship.

We are to be sanctified—set apart—to God. In truth, all our performances and most common actions are to reflect God. For that to be possible, our hearts have to be renewed, changed, and focused on the Savior. While others and you also desire to see outward changes to your circumstances, God is concerned with the state of the heart. Can you and I worship even while we stand in the midst of the rubble that the crisis has left behind? We can. It is not easy but worship is the place to begin. Worship does not put your life back together. Worship to the one and only God is what holds you together.

How can something as horrible as a crisis that has left a life in ruin reflect God? It is not the crisis that is to reflect God but it is your life, my life, the life of the one that has been changed by crisis. A life changed by crisis is fragile. A life changed by crisis is weak. A life changed by crisis is tired. A life changed by crisis feels invisible and exposed at the same time.

Dear one, it is through worship that the fragile are strengthened, the tired find rest, the invisible is seen, and the exposed is covered. This worship is the quiet personal moments that only you and

1   *Matthew Henry's Complete Commentary on the Bible.* Retrieved June 8, 2013, from http://studylight.org/com/mhm/view.cgi?bk=15&ch=3.

your Savior know. There are tears I have cried that only he has seen. The heart that breaks silently around others is deafening to the one who carries the broken heart. The Lord hears the breaking. He gathers the pieces. During those sleepless nights when you long for rest and feel frustrated because the one thing you need will not come, trust him and keep trusting. He gives sweet rest. Even that is in his timing.

Rest

Jesus said, "Come unto me, all who labor and are heavy laden, and I will give you rest" (Matthew 11:28, ESV). So often I found myself focusing on the word "rest" until I understood that I needed to act on the first word, "come." There had to be the place I continued to come back to, and time when I would consistently "come" to him. The only thing that would give me rest was the constant coming to the One who promised me rest. I had to come trusting that the rest would be given even when the task to rebuild overwhelmed.

At times, worship seems difficult because it requires the soul to be still (Psalm 46:10a). We can worship in different ways: through music, serving others, giving, or anything that brings us before the Lord. There is something to be said for when you and I worship the Lord from the depths of our soul with the time and talents that he has given us.

Stillness is so difficult when there is so much to do and accomplish. When you live with a crisis you want more than anything to live without it. However, you cannot get beyond it if you do not *do* something; yet worship requires stillness of soul. The very One who requires our soul to be still is the only One who can direct our steps to move forward. If we rush to rebuild our life after a crisis it is done in our own strength and will not stand. When we wait on the Lord and he renews our strength (Isaiah 40:31), we can place our trust in his perfect timing to rebuild what is broken. Choosing to worship in the midst of your shattered life is a hard battle to fight. As much as I don't like to admit this, the temptation to not worship is sometimes very inviting. There may be times when you have found yourself pulling away because your pain was great and, in a weird way, your pain had become comfortable. Worship before Jehovah-Rapha, the God Who Heals (Exodus 15:26), is realizing that the pain is being peeled away, and that you are becoming completely exposed. It is so difficult to be fully aware of your pain. Awareness of pain can be more painful than merely feeling pain. If you are never completely aware then maybe you never have to completely feel. Therein lies the dilemma for anyone finding himself at the crossroads of decision: to remain a life in crisis, or become a life changed by his grace. Becoming that person who begins to rebuild and lives life beyond the crisis only happens by living in complete awareness of the pain. By being aware of the pain one can then truly begin to see the goodness of the Lord. Nehemiah was told of the devastation of his homeland, yet it wasn't until he was in the middle of the mess that he was completely aware of the distress they were in. He saw the ruins. He heard the despair of the people's heart. He understood the complexity of the circumstances. It is the same with your heart. You can simply acknowledge your life is not as it should be, or you can be responsive to the circumstances by expressing your heart's pain, seeing what has been ruined, feeling the depth of hurt and loss, and seeking understanding from God.

The Blessings of Worship

I am so thankful that I made the choice to worship. Months into my crisis, I was reminded and my heart renewed when I heard the lyrics in "Everlasting," a song by Andy Chrisman: "I am confident that I will see the goodness of the Lord." It became a prayer that I would repeat over and over. I repeated those words so much to hear them, to reassure my heart, to choose to trust that *God is good*. I began to realize that he is good no matter if my life fits neatly and is beautifully packaged, or if it lies in ruins, others judge, some turn on me, and everything around me is an ugly mess. He is good.

Psalm 27 was the nourishment I gave to my weary soul. "Wait for the Lord; be strong, and let your heart take courage; wait for the Lord" (Ps. 27:14, ESV). This is the key to having the momentum to begin rebuilding, and then the stamina to continue rebuilding: the perfect balance of waiting while you worship. Determine to not get ahead of God, and focusing on remaining in him. John 15 commands us to abide in Christ. Abiding is continuing to be present. As long as I continue to be present in Christ, abiding in him, it is difficult for me to get ahead of him. It is also impossible for me to lag behind. Abiding in Christ provides the hope as I wait for him. I can hope for him and through him to restore what is broken.

Rebuild with the understanding that he does not negotiate his terms. He is authority. He sustains you. He gives the increase. He takes away. He is God. He is preeminent. HE IS! The purpose to rebuilding our lives is not to reflect what you or I want. The purpose is to reflect him. It is to bring him glory. It is to rebuild our lives in such a way that God shines through and in the end the legacy left points others to the saving grace of Jesus Christ.

With this understanding, why do we struggle? For me, each new sunrise proved the long road ahead would not be easy. Every time I faced a judgmental attitude from someone I trusted most, a newly revealed lie, lack of sleep and hurting jaw due to intense teeth grinding, and a grocery store trip with just a few dollars to feed myself and my children, I had to give myself the pep talk of my life.

I had to go back to my values. I had to step back and try to see the big picture, the one that was framed with integrity, faith, trust, and truth. I had come to realize that what held the fragile frame of my so-called life was, and is, worship.

Maybe you have recently left the graveside of a loved one and your grief is greater than you can carry. Maybe you are still staring at the pen you held as you signed unwanted divorce papers. Maybe you fret over a checking account that cannot deliver, and you feel anxious about which needs can be met when you have so little. Maybe you just cannot stomach the thought of more waiting in a doctor's office as you continue treatment for the disease that holds your body hostage. Maybe the pain of the abuse you have suffered at the hands of evil is emotionally paralyzing. Whatever the details are that sum up your crisis, those details are important. However, you are most important. Let the rebuilding of your life begin with your worship of the One who makes no mistakes. He allowed this into your life. He is the lifter of your head (Psalm 3:3) and when you gaze upon him the details of your crisis will dim in the light of his glory. You will be given strength in him, through him and by him. You will trust his purpose. You will be changed by him.

As I was growing up, my mother would often say to me and my brother, "What is in the well will come up in the bucket." I don't know if that statement was her adapted version of Jesus' declaration in Matthew 15:18 that "what comes out of the mouth proceeds from the heart, and this defiles a person" (ESV). Regardless, my mother made her point.

A crisis will draw from your well so much deeper each time that you will be exhausted. Everything within you will come up and come out. It is only in worship and through worship that our dry well is replenished with the living water that guarantees we will never thirst again.

I realized, as maybe you are too, that all my ugly came up in the bucket. My heart, the part of me that has no good (Romans 7:18), the part of me that is so deceitful even I cannot know it (Jeremiah 17:9), was revealed more and more. Most of the time I was the only one, other than the Lord, who knew these things about me. I am sure it is the same with you. Alone with your thoughts, you become keenly aware of your need for a redeemer and time spent in worship. Will you be courageous and lay yourself on the altar of worship, die to self, and live in Christ?

CHAPTER FIVE

The Valley of Danger

Standing Strong with Weak Emotions

"God, the Lord, is my strength; he makes my feet like the deer's; he makes me tread on my high places" (Habakkuk 3:19, ESV). I wrote this verse in my journal on one of my darkest days. When you live in a crisis there are so many dark days that you are never really sure when one begins and one ends. I quickly realized, as I am sure you have also, that the emotions we wrestle with drain us more than the reason for our crisis. Nehemiah and the people of Jerusalem rebuilt the Valley Gate, which of course overlooked a valley. This word "valley" means a steep valley, narrow gorge. In other words, this valley was not easily traveled. That doesn't mean impossible to travel, but the mental picture is of a difficult journey with potential complications.

To be honest, I was not prepared for the unexpected turn of events that landed me in a valley of unpredictable emotions. I finally understood King David's words in Psalm 23: "Even though I walk through the valley of the shadow of death...." Most of my life I had heard those words at funerals. I wasn't dead, though. I was very much alive and I felt every pulse of my broken heart. As I thought through "shadow of death," I began focusing on just that one word: *shadow.* A crisis, at some point, leads you directly into a steep valley full of unpredictable emotional shadows.

Control

The danger of emotions that cannot be predicted is the desire for control. The more you try to control and the harder you fight for control, the more you lose control. You fight the criticism you face. Maybe you have tried every way possible to explain yourself and find yourself continually misunderstood. You desire more than anything to be heard but everything you say seems to fall on deaf ears. You want to be accepted as you are, a complete mess, and very few if any can be comfortable with that. One of my greatest struggles was in needing support. The discouragement that made things darker came in discovering that people I should have been able to lean on had either become distant or removed themselves completely. In situations like this, you find yourself alone and weary, standing in the dark shadows of emotions that scare you. Then hope peaks through the darkness and you dare to hope.

As followers of Christ we are to develop self-control (Galatians 5:22). When life is unraveling, the tendency is to be more focused on trying to control things or others. We can't control other people and there will be certain things that remain beyond control. I can't control what others think, assume, or the opinions they have about my divorce. I can't force or manipulate long-term circumstances to work in my favor. I also cannot control through ignoring my circumstances or living in denial. Control rooted in forcing the circumstances of my crisis to make me feel more comfortable will only lead to isolation. This type of control does not allow for others to help you. It actually discourages others. When we grip tightly to this ever-promising type of control we are less likely to listen to truth and to entrust our circumstances to the Lord. We become more miserable and lonelier.

This all began in the Garden of Eden and has continued throughout time. Satan convinced Adam and Eve to eat the fruit. Until they were tempted, Adam and Eve were content to live within the boundaries and freedom God had given them. Living in the freedom of God's control is safe. As we know, once Adam and Eve took matters into their own hands everything as they knew it unraveled. Life became hard.

Sarah (Sarai) took control because of unbelief and offered Hagar to Abram (Genesis 16). Saul thought he could be in control and offered the sacrifice out of impatience (1 Samuel 15). Samson thought his great might gave him control and he made wrong choices (Judges 14–16). The rich, young ruler seemed to want to follow Christ but went away sad because it would mean giving up all he did control (Luke 18:18–23). How often do you and I think we are or want to be in control? Yet, our control is motivated from selfish desires and the hopes of selfish gain. Unbelief motivated Sarah, impatience enticed Saul to do something that was not his responsibility or his right. Self-reliance led Samson to make wrong choices, and worldly comfort outweighed eternal security for the rich, young ruler. We too are tempted to take control of our circumstances and are easily led astray by our selfish motives.

Surrender

Surrendering our need to be in control and confessing the motives that tempt us will lead us to experience the safety of living within God's control. Surrender will lead to trusting and the willingness to take steps as the Lord directs. Moses walked in between walls of water at the Red Sea. Joshua walked around the wall of Jericho. Jonah was vomited up from the large fish. Nehemiah rebuilt the walls of Jerusalem in fifty-two days. Esther spoke up and saved her people. Peter stepped out of the boat and walked on water. Paul and Silas praised the Lord in prison, and God sent the earthquake to release them. What would have happened if any of these people had not surrendered?

Isaiah 55:8 states clearly, "For my thoughts are not your thoughts, neither are your ways my ways, declares the Lord" (ESV). If ever there is an antidote to my control issues, this is it. The Lord's plans are not my plans and the manner in which he does things is not the way I would do them. I had to humble myself and admit that I strive to control. Confessing I don't trust the Lord's plans and his ways was the first of many steps to fully live. Again, living in the unknown of a crisis, the truths of a holy, all-knowing God reveal my distrust and lack of faith.

Surrendering to full trust that the Lord knew best and was completely aware of my pain gave insight to my selfish motives. Relinquishing and confessing this opened the doors of my heart to live in the control of the God who is all wise. Letting go of my way of doing things is always a great challenge. At times, it requires more courage to let go than to hang on. It is in the letting go that we have the ability to reach for Jesus and experience his strength.

Shadows

As I read further, I learned more extensive definitions of this word "shadow." I was relieved that there is no substantial evil in it. This gave me more courage to deal with my emotions instead of being too afraid to deal with them. Therein lies a dangerous denial. I remember as a child feeling afraid of the shadows in my dark bedroom. Lying in bed, I would be completely gripped by fear because the shadow had my imagination running wild. As a parent, I have seen this happen to my own children. What a relief when we, together, are able to know what is making the shadow. Finding the tree branch outside, the toy sitting on the shelf, or the piece of furniture cast by the light of a bright moon. Knowing what is real and what causes certain things to seem so terrifying will ease fear, if not dissipate it all together.

Emotions are tricky. In the moment emotions seem reliable and then as time passes, emotions change and you find yourself realizing that you can't completely trust your emotions. When the emotions you have are a result of profound hurt, grief, shock, or damage, the sting of those emotions is frightening. At the onset of your crisis you might want to deny and claim things are not as bad as they are. By coping through denial, you have a false sense of security. The grip of fear is mistakenly eased by the deception of denial. The million dollar question to ask yourself, "What am I afraid of?"

Nehemiah chose to not live in denial. In chapter 2, he took a long look at the damage. As hard as it must have been for him to take in the devastation, he knew that really seeing the situation was necessary. I don't know the details of your crisis or why you are reading this book. If you are in a crisis that has changed everything as far as you can see, I want to encourage you to look at the damage. Don't just know the damage is there. Know what the damage is. Put a name on it. For the people of Jerusalem, the words placed on the damage were "trouble," "shame," "disgrace," "burned," and "broken." Maybe it was the descriptive words that Nehemiah heard that deepened his grief. When he inquired about his homeland would his response be the same had he been given a vague answer? Sometimes I wonder if we create a shallow response to our crisis because we don't tell how it truly is. I am so grateful that the counselors, psychologist, and close friends who provided me with wisdom and support encouraged me to name the crisis. By sharing our crisis aloud, we not only sense the urgency; we also open our hearts to hope, and the possibility of rebuilding, renewal, and restoration.

I remember sitting with my small group as the couple who led the group gently urged me to share that I was separated from my husband. I hated hearing those words come out of my mouth. I hated saying the word "separated." It seemed to describe the uncertainty of our situation too much. Stating my circumstances by using one word was too uncomfortable for me because I was completely exposed. The word "separated" didn't give an answer nor did it seem to give direction. But that evening—and the days and weeks that turned into months—were some of the sweetest times I have had with a group of people because of the way they prayed for me and with me. Naming my circumstance was their invitation into my place of pain. They sensed the urgency and they responded with love, acceptance, and genuine concern. Each of them also protected my privacy. It was then that I had more courage to survey the damage of my crisis and I decided I would not sugarcoat it.

Anger

Anger has been an emotion I have wrestled with most of my life. I wouldn't say I have a short fuse, but anger over injustice can consume my thoughts. I don't like to be mistreated and I really don't like to see others mistreated. I have never quite found that balance of holding my tongue when I need to and speaking up when I need to. I seem to hold my tongue too long and when I have had enough, I lose my cool. I can come completely unglued. I feel the sting of the pain and I am not always prepared for it. If you are or have been through a life-changing crisis you know that I am not talking about anger that ends with losing your temper and saying things you will forever regret. I am talking about an anger that is more about the situation—those times when you can be mostly angry with yourself. There were times when that anger was beneficial. I would say things during counseling sessions and my counselor would help me work it out, wrestle with the thoughts and feelings and get a proper perspective. Other times, I would be corrected by a close Christian friend because the anger I felt was beginning to look more like bitterness.

God in his mercy kept sending me back to Nehemiah. There it was, Nehemiah 2:10: "But when Sanballat the Horonite and Tobiah the Ammonite servant heard this, it displeased them greatly that someone had come to seek the welfare of the people of Israel." And then in verse 19: "But when Sanballat the Horonite and Tobiah the Ammonite servant and Geshem the Arab heard of it, they jeered at us and despised us and said, 'What is this thing that you are doing? Are you rebelling against the king?'" (ESV). Nehemiah, the one we all applaud for taking on a task bigger than he was, did so with boldness and tenacity. Usually, Nehemiah is the one person used to get church members fired up about a building campaign. In all the times I had heard the story of Nehemiah, I had never paid attention to the potential danger of judgment, discouragement, and misunderstanding. These mindsets and heart attitudes are giant shadows that loom huge in the valley of life's devastation.

These three attitudes that anyone can face from others seem to be the shadows that loomed over my heart as I stumbled through the deep valley of my grief and my pain. I realized that there will be at least one person who makes it his or her personal mission to prevent your wounds from completely healing. Why? Why do these people think it is all right to speak harsh words? Can't they see that every step taken toward healing and restoration is extremely difficult? Their attitudes affect you and your emotions. My emotions became as unpredictable as the timing of their harsh judgment. The anger that I felt lasted longer than it ever should have. I was angry that others were judging me. Being judged and feeling judged became so unbearable that I wondered if it was possible for someone already broken to break more. Friend, I have been told I am not praying enough. I have been scolded that I need to be reading my Bible more. I have been told that my ministry to others would not be as effective. I have been told that I wasn't trying hard enough. (I'm feeling angry all over again just typing this!)

The shadows faced in the valley overwhelm. You may be desperately wanting, like me, just one good day. In an emotional sense, I desired to see blue sky, feel warm sunshine and feel "normal." Instead, the shadows were dark and at times grew darker. I just had to keep reminding myself that the Lord was present with me. About that time, Psalm 23 became more than just verses read at a funeral.

The Shepherd's Care

When you find yourself in the throes of a crisis, you feel disoriented; you need a GPS to know which way is up and which way is down. Sometimes, you might need someone to help you think. The stress brought about by a crisis kills brain cells. I am sure of it (OK, even if it's not a fact)! I could feel the toll especially impacting my ability to focus. Maybe you feel scattered, as I did. Maybe you realize, as I did, that you have little tolerance for general, shallow prayers. Let me share with you my re-discovery of Psalm 23. It was not only a relief to discover this truth tucked away in a well-known psalm, it was clear direction in how I was to pray for myself.

When I learned the purpose of the shepherd's rod and staff, I laughed out loud. Shepherds used their staffs for several purposes. Many times a shepherd would hold his rod out and as the sheep passed under he would count his sheep. Other times, a shepherd would use the staff to drive away anything that could scatter the sheep. This discovery unearthed a small treasure that was significant to my restoration. The good Shepherd, my Savior, has his rod over me. He counts me! He knows where I am at all times. He knows where I am physically. He also knows where I am emotionally. During this particular time, I was all over the place. However, he knew where every piece of my broken heart was, and he knew how to find the pieces and put them all back together.

My Shepherd also used his staff to drive away what could scatter me. I did lack mental focus. I mean, who doesn't when your life has fallen apart? For example, maybe you have found yourself at the grocery store check-out, proud of actually going shopping, only to realize after every item has been rung up and bagged that you do not have your wallet. Maybe you have forgotten to pick a child up from practice. Maybe you have left the house and come home hours later to find the television on, the flat iron smoking, and the hot but near-empty coffee pot burning that tiny bit of remaining liquid. I have done all of those things. It is amazing that I didn't burn our house down. Why? Heartbreak will bring on a scattered brain faster than it takes a cheetah to catch the gazelle.

To discover that the gentle Shepherd not only knew where I was at all times in every way possible, but would drive anything away that could scatter me, gave me peace beyond my own understanding. What a comfort to know you can ask the Lord to drive away your scattered emotions and help you focus. I hope that you will pray that for yourself and gain a deeper understanding that he knows right where you are. He knows you have just left the graveside of a child you can't imagine life without but are now forced to live life without. He knows you just left a lawyer's office and the divorce you now face is devastating. He knows the chemo treatments you must endure scare you and the reality of living with cancer scares you more. He knows you have all the hopes of bringing your perfect bundle of dreams into the world and the doctor's words were not what you expected, so you ask yourself if you are really a person who can raise a child with special needs. The job you were so secure in no longer exists, but he knows the anxiety you experience. You're facing all those unknowns that come with moving, and you never even planned to make the move. Friend, he is already where you will be going. Crisis comes with "what ifs" and "what now" and "who can help" questions. It sends us in many directions at one time. We are scattered and we are broken and our life is in a bazillion pieces. The gentle Shepherd knows. He knows more than you and I know. He has his eye on me and you.

I encourage you to ask the Lord daily, multiple times a day, to help your scattered emotions. He will. I began to pray specifically and he helped me focus. He gave me creative ideas to make me aware I at least had ducks, even if they weren't in a row. I am over three years into my crisis and my ducks are still not in a row, but I have let go of any expectation that they ever will be. I am simply thankful that God settles my mind. He really does keep us in perfect peace whose mind is fixed on him.

CHAPTER SIX

Unchanging Truth

Harnessed by Faith

Life falls apart. You wake up and hours later as you climb back into your bed you know a crisis hit your life and you will never be the same. You are in an emotional free fall. Your head is still spinning from the last several days and hours during which you saw your life completely change. You know you have been freefalling, and then there is a moment when you realize someone is holding you. You will not be destroyed.

Several years ago, I sat at the funeral of Ryan, a young man full of life, laughter and dreams. His life—from our perspective—had been cut short. The big smile, magnetic personality, and funny antics had been silenced. At the end of the funeral, after the great truth of the Gospel had been presented and some had decided to follow the same Jesus Ryan now worships in person, it was time for the final song. "Amazing Grace" would have been perfect. The service could have ended with the familiar song "I Can Only Imagine." As Ryan's body was rolled out of the auditorium and I could not stop the tears, I stood there with the thousand other friends that loved Ryan and his family. I looked over to Ryan's mother and father, who had no answers or understanding of the senseless tragedy but with arms raised and their voices lifted toward Heaven sang the lyrics to Matt Redman's song "You Never Let Go":

> Oh no, you never let go
> Oh no, you never let go
> Through the calm and through the storm
> Oh no, you never let go
> In every high and every low
> Oh no, you never let go
> Lord, you never let go of me

Maybe that is you. I know it has and on some days still is me. Clinging to something I cannot see. Faith. When anxiety overwhelms my spirit, I remind myself, "You never let go Lord, you never let go."

Anchored in Christ

I found a treasure years ago while digging into God's Word. To be honest, this is one of those profound treasures I did not realize until my own crisis hit that I would need as much as I need gravity. Hebrews 6:17-19a told me:

> So when God desired to show more convincingly
> to the heirs of the promise the unchangeable character

of his purpose, he guaranteed it with an oath, so that by two unchangeable things, in which it is impossible for God to lie, we who have fled for refuge might have strong encouragement to hold fast to the hope set before us. We have this as a sure and steadfast anchor of the soul…

When a crisis storms into your life it changes the landscape of your life. The only thing you want is for everything to return to the way it was and remain the same. But no matter how hard you try to make everything stay the same, you cannot. My dear friends will have to try to make a life without Ryan, but they can never go back to life with Ryan alive. You can't "go back." You can't "make life" the same anymore. You can't, you can't, you can't.

Everything has changed and we long for something that will not ever change. We not only want but we desperately need something that will be the same every morning and every evening. Tucked in Hebrews 6, there is a truth that God desires to show me and to show you. Not only does he want to show us, he sets out to convince us. He will do what it takes to convince me and you that the "unchangeable character of his purpose is guaranteed." This word "unchangeable" means fixed and unalterable. I really cannot wrap my head around this. Has anyone ever experienced something that is fixed and unalterable? We live in a world that thrives off change and altering things to make them better, more convenient, and more useful.

When crisis hits hard, the comfort found in that truth is like fresh air. Knowing the same El Roi who met Hagar in the desert is the God Who Sees *Me*. Realizing the same Jehovah-Shammah found in Ezekiel is the same God, the Lord is there. Resting in Jehovah Rapha, the Lord that heals will heal hearts—your heart and my heart. God has not changed. God cannot change. Everything else can and will change. Maybe this is one of the purposes for crisis, to begin to understand and accept change and when everything has changed and fallen apart, you find the only ONE who is unchanging desires for us to know him.

A crisis sometimes gives us the crazy notion to run. We think, *If I could just run away then maybe it wouldn't be as it is and maybe my heart would stop hurting.* I don't know why we think this way. Yet, tucked inside Hebrews that mindset is acknowledged. "Who have fled for refuge." When everything is changing and you know you can never go back to the way life was before, you just want to feel safe. Life B.C. (Before Crisis) seems like a dream and you now live in life A.D. (After Devastation). It just seems logical to want to flee, to run hard, to find somewhere safe and never be hurt again. God knew it when the writer of Hebrews put pen to paper, and God understands that now. So he gives us himself to run to and nothing to hold onto except hope. I have gripped hope the last several years and I am sure there are marks showing the places where you have dug your fingers in deep, gripping with all your might. I have also left marks on hope. A crisis will do that. It will give you a grip that others do not understand. But you get tired of gripping hard. Gripping hope can be tiresome and sometimes painful. What happens if you slip and let go of hope? Our humanity has a way of giving out. What then? Herein lies the real truth. We do not hold hope; hope holds us.

"A sure and steadfast anchor of the soul." A life in crisis needs "sure and steadfast." If the truth of the anchor is like oxygen to my lungs, then knowing and experiencing that anchor as sure and steadfast is like an oxygen mask; once I apply it, I will have relief in my struggle. "Sure" is firm and can be relied on. "Steadfast" is stable. I need stable! I must have something to rely on. This "anchor of the soul" brought me to a place where I could say, "It is well with my soul." The word "anchor" used in Hebrews means "safeguard." Then I held this truth under the light of God's grace and found that there was even more depth to this word. It related to the way in which, for many years, anchors were made like an upside down T. When dropped into the deep waters of the sea they would drag the bottom until they caught onto something. There was no immediate hold. It was learned that if the bottom of an anchor was angled it would sink to the bottom, dig deep into the ocean bed, and hold immediately, not letting loose. Not only had I discovered an engineering lesson in Scripture, but also a truth that brought a deep sense of safety. At salvation, God anchored my soul. Storms will come, crisis will threaten, but I cannot be swept away because I am held. I am held by the anchor that has dug so deep into grace that nothing can dig it out. No storm can loosen it and no crisis can move it. I am anchored!

Resting In His Ways

I wonder what the conversation was like as Nehemiah and the people rebuilt the Old Gate at Jerusalem. This gate was the place where the elders met to discuss community issues and make judgments. The spiritual application of this gate speaks of the old paths and the old truths. We are told in Jeremiah 6:16 to "stand by the roads, and look, and ask for the ancient paths, where the good way is; and walk in it, and find rest for your souls" (ESV). As they rebuilt this gate, did they talk about the good old days? Did they talk about the hopes they had of their "new" city? Did they recite the truths of the scriptures?

A crisis produces a deep longing to rest. Not the rest that sleep promises but the rest of the soul. The only way to have that kind of rest is to walk in the truths of God's Word. You may not understand why this crisis has come into your life. Or, maybe you do know and that knowledge has made it all the more devastating. Whatever your crisis is, and why it has happened, there is rest for your soul. You don't have to wring your hands. You can stop pacing. You can stop worrying. You can find the opportunity for joy and laughter. You can rest. How? Just as Jeremiah instructed us: you stand, you see, you ask, you walk.

You stand firm in his redemptive work in your life through the blood of Christ. This work, "stand" means to stand still, stop moving and doing, cease. I needed to understand this principle for myself, and I want to encourage you to learn it as well. *Matthew Henry's Complete Commentary of the Bible* explains it best: "[God] would have [the Israelites] to consider, not to proceed rashly, but to do as travellers in the road, who are in care to find the right way which will bring them to their journey's end, and therefore pause and enquire for it"[2].

I think it is safe to say that most of us in the midst of a crisis have a deep desire to make the right choices and do the right things. The challenge is to "not proceed rashly." In other words, we must be extremely attentive to our souls, so that we do not become careless and impetuous. Carelessness can be a result of fatigue. It can also be a result of an ungrateful heart. Can gratefulness be an active attitude in the individual's life which has come undone? Can the fatigue of the soul be so real that one makes impulsive decisions with hopes to ease if not heal the pain? Yes.

Carelessness can get the best of us sometimes. It did for Moses in Numbers 20. Moses struck the rock instead of speaking to the rock as the Lord had explicitly directed. Moses gave into frustration and he was careless with the Lord's instruction. Sometimes we can crave relief from the circumstances so much that we overlook the

---

2   Retrieved June 8, 2013, from http://studylight.org/com/mhm/view. cgi?bk=23&ch=6.

moment-by-moment importance of trusting God's best in every way he may direct us.

Numbers 11 also gives a vivid story of ungratefulness and its results. Hardship can bring out the worst in us at times. God's people had seen God's power and were experiencing his care and provision daily. However, the everyday wear and tear of hardship can put us in the place to give in to carelessness. The beginning of the end began with ungratefulness. Ungratefulness will affect others and ungratefulness is not an attitude you can keep to yourself. Manna was given to the Israelites daily, in amounts sufficient to meet each day's needs. The Lord had daily given the Israelites what they needed to sustain them. Yet, they wanted to eat something different. The complaining took root and developed an ungratefulness that affected everyone around them, including Moses. However, God gave the Israelites what they wanted. Knowing that it would be no good to them and it would not bring satisfaction, the Lord gave them what they asked for. Not only did the Lord give them what they wanted but he gave them more than they wanted. They became sick with what they had begged for. The result was that the selfish desire led to their physical deaths. There are times when, if we are not careful, we will be driven by ungratefulness and receive what we want. Our wants will never satisfy. But accepting how the Lord meets our needs will always satisfy and sustain us.

The psalmist wrote a brief reflection on Numbers 11 and summed it up best in Psalm 106:15: "And he gave them their request, but sent leanness into their soul" (NKJV). I understand the weariness of living every day in crisis mode. I understand the longing of your heart to want something and anything other than what you have right now. However, I hope you realize that the Lord is the only one who sustains you. He is giving you exactly what you need to bring you to the place of healing. He is providing for you in the midst of your great pain. Resist the temptation to complain, and become ungrateful. Instead, press on and pursue him who will fatten your soul with the truth of his Word. Stand firm in the promises of the God who can and will provide for you.

Pause

It is during the times I have come to call "pressing pause" that you can see the fruit. The work of rebuilding is daily. There are times that you have to make yourself press pause and look around your life to see what work has been accomplished. Sometimes you may have to look harder than other times, but the fruit is there and it is growing. You see the fruit that is growing in the deepest churned places of your heart. As you begin to look at all the areas of your life that are affected by your crisis, I hope you are seeing the goodness of the Lord. Sometimes his goodness is exaggerated and others can see it too. Other times, it is small and meant only for you. Maybe you are realizing that seeds have been planted and there are things growing in your life that only God could cultivate. A longing for him like you have never had beckons you to abide in him. Even in great sadness, you are experiencing the joy of the Lord. You are now seeing in the darkest moments that you have already experienced his peace that does surpass your understanding. This gives you hope that when dark times come again, you can rest in the peace that you know he will continue to provide every need.

When my children and I were preparing to move to another state, I was completely trusting that the Lord would provide us a house that would fit into my extremely small budget. However, a few days before we were to look for a house to rent, I was nervous and anxious. You see, I had found only one house that might fit our needs and my budget. Personally, I like options and would have felt better if I had several houses to view, but that wasn't possible. That night as I was tucking my son into bed, he confessed to me that he had not been praying for us to find a house. I teasingly asked him why not. I assumed that for my carefree boy, the concerns of a house were the last things on his mind. He replied, "I have only asked God to give me a creek." With tears in my eyes, I listened as he asked, "Is there a creek at this house we will go look at?" I paused and told him that in the description of the house it did mention a creek. He smiled a million dollar smile. I scooped him into my arms and said, "I hope you know that God cares about little boys and creeks." Each night we fall asleep listening to that wonderful bubbling creek, my Heavenly Father reinforces to my healing heart: "I know you. I know your children. I am healing and restoring you all." The creek near our house—which was our only option—has become my reminder to pause and see the goodness of the Lord.

I don't know everything you will notice when you press the pause button. It could be an unexpected call from a dear friend, the perfect encouragement you needed. You might find a small gift left for you on the front porch. It could be something as simple as a great bargain at your favorite store that enables you to save some money. You might receive a sweet note in your mailbox from a dear friend, and the words written like a direct hug from your Heavenly Father. I know that if you press pause you will see something about which you can confidently know: *That is the goodness of the Lord.*

You ask for wisdom and insight that comes through fearing the Lord. You walk in his ways with his Word lighting your path, guiding your next steps. This wisdom and this walk are done with great intention. Psalm 25:12, reminds us, "Who is the man who fears the Lord? Him will he instruct in the way that he should choose" (ESV). Likewise, Psalm 111:10 explains that the "fear of the LORD is the beginning of wisdom; all those who practice it have a good understanding. His praise endures forever!" (ESV). When you walk through your most difficult days with the wisdom and insight that comes only with fearing the Heavenly Father, he will give you instruction and understanding. This fear is not a state of living in terror; it is a continual state of awe and deep reverence.

This isn't a four step program; it is a way a life. It is how your life goes from crisis to credibility. Others will watch and wonder. You will be strengthened as your soul rests. When others ask you how you do it, you can say "I don't. I am anchored. My God has me and he has my crisis." You can be the face on the poster with the caption: "God's Got This—Harnessed by His Grace."

Let your life be rebuilt on the old truths of the unchanging God. He sees you. He has you. You can free fall into his grace. You can live fearlessly in the midst of the dangerous crisis that blows cold on your soul, because you know that your soul is anchored.

CHAPTER SEVEN

Exposed

Examined, Tried, and Proven

The relentless love of the almighty God has been covering what we cannot since the beginning of time. There is nothing more frightening than the feeling of being unsafe because of exposure. God has not only promised but has acted on our behalf to cover us. When he walked the garden looking for Adam and Eve, he came prepared to cover them not to condemn them (Genesis 3:21). When the Lord examines our hearts, it is always to cover with his grace and mercy through the blood of Jesus. He does not examine us to condemn and shame us. You and I can rest in the Lord, "For God did not send his Son into the world to condemn the world, but in order that the world might be saved through him" (John 3:17, ESV). I desire for you to understand and be able to identify what is of the Lord in the examining process of your crisis, and what is not of the Lord. Sometimes when we are trying to manage the pain our crisis inflicts, it can become difficult to know what pain has purpose and what pain will drain the life out of us. Understanding God's purpose for examining our hearts can only come through spending time in his Word. We also know that "…when we are judged by the Lord, we are disciplined so that we may not be condemned along with the world" (1 Corinthians 11:32, ESV).

To be exposed is to be uncovered. Grief exposes our every fear and reveals how helpless we really are. Fear of the unknown exposes the ugliness of how we fight to control and manipulate to make ourselves feel comfortable. Our fear of exposure lures us to minimize and to hide. Examination of our thoughts, actions, motives, words, and expressions are all bare. This is painful not because some question us, our circumstances, or our motives. It is painful because we are emotionally naked. It is easy to think there is no place to hide and no way to find cover.

Being examined makes me nervous. I am nervous because I do not like the feeling of being vulnerable. One day when I was about five years old I walked into the kitchen to ask my mother something, and suddenly I knew I was exposed. Standing there completely helpless in front of my mom and my grandmother, I saw that my skirt had left its place around my waist and lay at my ankles. The elastic popped and my tears rushed down my cheeks. I was completely exposed and thoroughly embarrassed. Maybe that is where the dread began. Whatever the reason, I hate it. Exposure is one of those experiences where, no matter how hard you try to cover and hide, you can never get out of it quickly enough. Others remember, and you certainly never forget. But what if there is a purpose to exposure? What if exposure is the only way to truly be hidden?

I struggle with the discipline to write in my journal daily. However, I am thankful that I do write and can look back on things that have shaped and re-shaped my heart over these last few years. I have read over and over one particular entry as a reminder and motivation to remain faithful. In this entry, I copied down Job 31:6: "Let me be weighed on honest scales, That God may know my integrity" (New King James Version). I added Psalm 26:2: "Examine me, O LORD, and prove me; Try my mind and my heart" (NKJV.) Then I wrote a prayer that began with the words, "I am entering through the Miphkad Gate. I am being inspected and judged."

Examined. Judged. These words are sharp; just hearing them can cause us to feel uneasy. At some point someone—maybe even you—will think it is a God-given right for others to examine your crisis and judge you. There were days during this time that I wondered how much more my heart could break. Judging of this kind seemed cruel and the examination of my crisis felt disrespectful. I didn't expect other brothers and sisters in Christ to be judgmental. Therefore I did not expect this to be part of the rebuilding process. I was naïve and that is what caused much of the hurt. Somehow it was necessary to the restoration process. The pain of being judged by others was unbearable. At certain points this can be more devastating than the crisis itself. Words are hurtful and people are careless with their words. I wish for you as I have wished for myself that I could forget some of the words I heard. I can't forget and I give them to my Heavenly Father for him to renew my mind with his truth. The judgment that comes from others can be hurtful or it can be a blessing. How can it be a blessing? You are more open to the Lord being your judge and I hope that you will choose to place yourself in the light of the all wise and kind judge, Jesus Christ.

The Appointed Place

This particular gate mentioned in Nehemiah 3, the Miphkad Gate, may have been used for trading animals to be utilized in sacrificial worship and it may have been the place where men were drafted into military service and people were counted for the census. The word "miphkad" means "inspection." As I studied, I learned this gate was an appointed place. There were some things and some people that had to pass through this gate.

Dear one, our crisis will require that we pass through the inspection. Those of us living in crisis will be examined by others and by the Lord. We will be looked over, looked into and judged. How do we know who is being used by the Lord for this process and who is not? Don't mistake the truth that stings for judgment rooted in wrong motives. Nathan confronted King David with truth that did sting (2 Samuel 12). The circumstances that led to the confrontation were displeasing to God. However, Nathan spoke truth completely motivated by love and a desire to see the king restored. When the Lord uses people in our lives to speak truth that is difficult for us to hear, it is for the purpose of our restoration. It should be spoken in love, presented with empathy for our circumstances and the clear desire to further our restoration. It is important to know who the safe individuals are that will walk through your crisis with you. Ask the Lord to give you discernment in knowing who these people will be.

Safety

It doesn't seem fair. If I could, I would walk with you through this. Not only would I cry with you but I would understand your tears. I understand your fear, your anger, your frustration, and your dread. However, God can use all of these for our restoration. A crisis is not a sudden free pass for no one to ever question or examine your life.

In fact, the crisis you are in may give all the more reason for you to be examined. This wasn't a principle I wanted to embrace. However, I went through it. It was as if I had been opened up for others to peer into my raw emotions, my embarrassing pain, and my bleeding wounds. Being examined is not pretty and what others see and expose is difficult to endure. There is no medication strong enough to ease that kind of pain, the throbbing pain of being judged.

How do you know who is safe and who is not safe to examine you in time of crisis? Safe people are individuals that will walk with you and at times guide you toward restoration. One of my dearest friends has not only walked with me through my crisis but she has been in my mess willingly. She said it best one day as we talked about knowing who in your life will evaluate your circumstances and speak loving truth to you, and who will judge you and bring only more harm. She said to me, "Joy, you're safe with the person who pulls the log out their own eye before taking the speck out of your eye." The safe person will understand that holding me to God's standards is the loving thing to do. Matthew 7:1–5 tells us:

> Judge not, that you be not judged. For with the judgment you pronounce you will be judged, and with the measure you use it will be measured to you. Why do you see the speck that is in your brother's eye, but do not notice the log that is in your own eye? Or how can you say to your brother, 'Let me take the speck out of your eye,' when there is the log in your own eye? You hypocrite, first take the log out of your own eye, and then you will see clearly to take the speck out of your brother's eye" (ESV).

It is clear from this passage that judging is a sin. However, to reprove a brother or sister in Christ is a duty. It is imperative that you and I know the difference. I would never want anyone to take advantage of your pain and judge you. Harming your already-broken heart would be cruel.

Often people will judge, holding to their own standards and preferences to make themselves feel better. Yet, there will be loving people who will be the voice of James 5:19–20: "My brothers, if anyone among you wanders from the truth and someone brings him back, let him know that whoever brings back a sinner from his wandering will save his soul from death and will cover a multitude of sins" (ESV). Dear one, if you have wandered away from the truth in your crisis then I hope there is someone pursuing you to bring you back to God's life-changing truth.

We are prone to wander. A crisis has the potential to detour our hearts away from the truth that will keep us. If we are not careful we can be uncomfortable with the word "judge" and go so far the opposite direction that we become unloving. In these verses James wrote, "if anyone among you wander from the truth and someone brings him back"—and there is a lot that takes place between "wanders from the truth" and "brings him back." The person who pursues the wandering one has recognized the movement away from Christ. Sometimes, the pain of our crisis is so deep that we pull away from Christ. The loving person who is removing the log out of their own eye is able to love unconditionally the one with the speck. This person will pursue your heart understanding what is at stake—your soul. This person does not judge you to condemn you. This person acts with a tough love and will take the time to understand you while never dismissing the reason you have wandered away. To bring you back means the reason you have wandered from the truth has to be confronted. The gracious person who brings you back from your wandering is never motivated by their preferences. They are loving you with God's standards.

On a hot, summer day I walked to my car completely discouraged because it seemed my life was beyond repair. I knew I had not wandered from the truth. I knew I was clinging to God's truth like a man overboard would cling to a lifeline. My belief in God and who God is had not changed. My beliefs dictated how I conducted myself, but my circumstances were being judged. The disgraceful details of my marriage were coming out and several people were uncomfortable. The harmful judgment was an attack on my circumstances and a complete dismissal of my character. The loving person who will judge you with kindness will always put your character above your circumstances. This deep hurt birthed insight and understanding that I did not have to entrust myself to these people. I only needed to entrust myself to my Heavenly Father.

While we do not have a physical Miphkad Gate and appointed place to walk through, we do have an appointed place, our heart. This place is the only place God examines. This is the place where he judges. Psalm 26:2 says, "Examine me, O Lord, and try me; Test my mind and my heart" (NASB). The word "examine" means to scrutinize and to prove, to make a trial. Isn't that what is in the eye of the storm called Crisis? The scrutiny and the trial we face. We seem to think the scrutiny is from others, whereas the psalmist is asking God to examine him. Do we really desire God to examine us and try us and test our mind and our heart? Having your crisis and your responses to your crisis judged by others can be awful. However, we must realize that if we are not careful we would put all our attention on what other people think about us and not pay attention to what God knows of us. When God's examination becomes most important and his results reveal truth then anything others say and think will not sting as badly. We are human. I came to the place where I was more concerned with what God knew of my heart than what people thought of me.

The Heart's Response

Integrity is a word easily thrown around, but difficult to live. A life in crisis is chaotic and for a Christian integrity is necessary to calm the chaos. In the beginning of a crisis it may be sheer panic, disbelief, tears, talking to anyone who will listen, and more tears. Suddenly the loneliness sets in and the chill it blows on your heart is startling. Loneliness can have a way of resurrecting every emotion you think you have quieted. Like a mirage in the desert, loneliness can draw you into thinking you have solutions to your problems when there never were any answers at all. It is an illusion.

Too many hurt by life-changing crisis underestimate the power of loneliness. As a counselor I had become a student to other people's pain. I listened and I learned. Like you, I never thought my life's crisis would ever be a disgrace. In the back of my mind I sometimes wondered if I would handle it well were I ever in "their shoes." Some people taught me what not to do and others inspired me as I walked with them through hurts, discouragement, and dismay. And then, I became a statistic. My life could be labeled, put in a column of failure and deep sadness, and forever changed. What now?

Job 31:6 became the needle on my compass and Psalm 26:2 became simple food that fed my soul. To make it through the examination process that is necessary to restoration, I encourage you to walk with integrity. In the end, that may be all you have.

"Let Him weigh me with accurate scales, and let God know my integrity" (Job 31:6, NASB). When Job determined in his heart to be a man of integrity, he must have understood that others would peer into his life and look for something, anything to explain away his great suffering. Others will do the same during your crisis response. It is important that you live life as unto the Lord. It matters. It is important that you make every decision, even the smallest ones, through the lens of integrity.

I cannot tell you what will be required of you from the Lord. I will share the small, practical decisions I made at the beginning of my crisis to walk in integrity. I would take the time to talk with at least one of my five closest friends daily. I needed the encouragement and I also wanted to be transparent with them about daily happenings. I canceled our cable for both practical and heart-related reasons. I did not want to waste away my time in the evenings watching mindless television. I also could not afford to put myself in a place of temptation to view things I should not see. When by myself in the car, I listened to sermons or Christian radio. I did not go into debt. I purposed in my heart to trust the Lord with my meager finances to provide all we needed. We did not miss church or time with the small group Bible study. Even though there has been so much rebuilt and restored since my crisis began, I continue to remain committed to my integrity before the Lord. I continue to stay in close weekly contact with these wonderful friends through phone calls and emails. I am completely aware of the amount of television time in our home, and it is very little time. I am so thankful for podcasts! I read books that challenge and encourage my walk with the Lord. Never underestimate the small decisions. Whether it is decisions that help you physically, spiritually, emotionally, or mentally—make sure each of those decisions helps you rebuild with integrity.

If integrity is one side of the coin then Psalm 26:2 is the other side. The American Standard Version says: "Examine me, O Jehovah, and prove me; Try my heart and my mind." If we surrender to God's scales and he weighs us then we must be at peace with how he chooses to examine our heart and mind. To be all right with one and try to manipulate the other is hypocritical. You can't have it your way and his way. You may have already entered into this area of your crisis. You may be living out the portion of these lyrics to the song "Restored (The Grindstone Song)" by Cheri Keaggy: "I've been living against the grindstone, where nothing is sure but the Lord." It is more crucial now than ever to understand and trust the Lord. There is purpose to your pain. There is reason for your heart being examined and your mind being tried.

This season of the rebuilding process is difficult. However, this season is for you. God wants to do something amazing in your life. He wants to remove what doesn't belong in your life and he wants to demolish what has held you down. If you want to rebuild and have your life restored, then work through the pain and trust your loving Heavenly Father, who is good to bring forth his purpose.

Discipline

The Lord's examination will lead to discipline. This discipline is for the purpose of instructing and teaching us. It is in the heart that we can experience a holy God who is the only just judge over our heart. 1 John 3:19–20 states, "By this we shall know that we are of the truth and reassure our heart before him; for whenever our heart condemns us, God is greater than our heart, and he knows everything" (ESV). It is comforting to know that God knows everything. *Matthew Henry's Complete Commentary of the Bible* explains this process: "Our heart here is our self-reflecting judicial power...This power can act as witness, judge, and executioner of judgment; it either accuses or excuses, condemns or justifies; it is set and placed in this office by God himself" [3]. What is wonderful about this explanation of our heart is the proclamation that 'God is greater than our heart.'"

God designed us with a conscience. He placed deep within our hearts the ability to judge and the need for justice. However, he is

---

3   Retrieved June 8, 2013, from http://studylight.org/com/mhm/view. cgi?bk=61&ch=3.

the righteous judge. He not only can know our actions; he is able to discern our motives.

Christy Nockels wrote the powerful words of "A Mighty Fortress." Every time I sing this song, I may be standing reverently on the outside but I am having a dance party on the inside. Pure, simple celebration motivated by a deep gratitude that I can never put into words. Nockels wrote:

> Our God is a consuming fire
> A burning holy flame, with glory and freedom
> Our God is the only righteous judge,
> Ruling over us with kindness and wisdom
> We will keep our eyes on you
> So we can set our hearts on you
> Lord, we will set our hearts on you!

Friend, if I could say one thing that will make a difference and change your perspective during this time of crisis and examination, I would repeat over and over that the God who is judging you is doing so with loving kindness and perfect wisdom. Hebrews 4:13 emphasizes, "And no creature is hidden from his sight, but all are naked and exposed to the eyes of him to whom we must give account" (ESV). He knows every detail of your crisis and he knows the devastation of your heart. However, our heart change is of more importance than the circumstances. He knows that when we are tested and examined, and when our heart is transformed by his truth, then we can see our crisis as the perfect opportunity for joy.

Just when you think you cannot endure the pain of exposure, El Roi (the God Who Sees) covers you with his grace, mercy, and love. Maybe your crisis is a consequence to sin in your life. His blood washes over your soul bringing forgiveness of sins. Maybe the crisis that devastated your heart does not have rhyme or reason from your perspective. You have his undivided attention. Maybe you find yourself in the ruins of crisis and you know you did everything in your power to stop it. He is there with you.

He will not allow you to pass through the examination process alone. To abandon us in our most vulnerable state would be cruel and unkind when we cry out to him and invite him into it. These characteristics cannot inhabit the holy God. We see in Daniel 3 that he did not abandon the Hebrew men when throne in the furnace. Instead, he walked in the fire with them. The fire could not consume them because God's presence consumed everything that would threaten their wellbeing. God did not leave Esther to go alone before her king uninvited, instead he protected her (Esther 5). When the adulterous woman was brought before the Savior, the salvation he gave her was larger than any stone that could have been hurled at her (John 8). The same God who walked in the fire, protected Esther, and covered the woman's sin with forgiveness is the same God who will remain with you as you are being examined.

CHAPTER EIGHT

Trust

Obedience Leads to Clarity

Every day for four years, I placed an eye patch over my son's eye with complete trust. To be honest, it was probably more hope for me and trust for him. I hoped that the doctor's orders would give my son better eyesight, and my son trusted that the doctor and I knew what we were doing. Four years after learning of his poor sight in his left eye, the results were in. Success! However, his eyesight isn't perfect. His left eye has improved, but he is still dependent on glasses to help him see. Wearing the patch never guaranteed complete healing of the eyesight. It only promised the possibility of a healthier eye. If we are not careful, we'll want a guarantee that we will not have struggles, or if we do they will be minor and short-lived. We prefer life be simple problems with simple fixes, such as: *Take this pill for the next ten days and you will be healed. Do these eight steps and you will have financial success. Attend marriage counseling for the next six weeks and all your problems will go away. Take your family to church every Sunday and no problems will come your way.* A crisis is the reality check that no one is exempt and no one can avoid life-altering events. For some, the crisis is seen by many; for others, the crisis is not as easy to detect. The public crises usually get most of the attention, but know that no matter how publically known or privately felt, there is one principle that applies to all, obedience.

Knowing the Comforter

The Fountain Gate is first mentioned in Nehemiah 2:14, when Nehemiah took his nighttime ride to survey the city and take in all the destruction. This gate led to the King's Pool. This same Fountain Gate is mentioned indirectly in the book of John. It is the place where Jesus healed a blind man.

Jesus' approach to bring healing to this blind man was unconventional, to say the least (John 9). I wonder how much the blind man knew of Jesus' ingredients of saliva and sand before he felt the mud cover his eyes. Jesus did not need saliva, dirt, or the pool in order to heal the man. When Jesus speaks, that is power. Nothing can be added to what already is everything: all powerful, all knowing, I AM, the beginning and the end, the way, the truth, and the life. But on this day, near the pool of Siloam, Jesus was creative. Jesus gave this man physical sight, but there was something greater at stake: the heart of this man. Once his eyesight was given to him, would his heart's sight be made clear?

We are sometimes tempted to try to make life go back to normal once you feel the crisis is over. This is human. Since the beginning of time, we find men and women promising God, bargaining with God, and living for God when the winds of crisis blow. A crisis creates desperation. Shallow Christians who have roots dug in only comfort-deep will be determined to make it through the crisis by the grace of God. During the crisis these people are only concerned with their comfort and when will they be comfortable again. In other words, if we are not careful, we will be desperate because of the circumstances and we won't be desperate for Christ. Desiring comfort can become our god, and we never know the Comforter. To know the Comforter you have to be patient with the pain. The person who desires to be comfortable over knowing the Comforter chooses not to recognize the purpose of the pain. It is so easy to mask the pain with entertaining nights, fun relationships, relaxing with drinks, that next pill, one more hour under the covers to forget the outside world. The heart that does not know the Comforter is determined—determined to be comfortable by shallow experiences and self-absorbed definitions.

The person who is desperate to know the Comforter comes to understand that nothing is in his or her time. Life after the crisis can never be like the one before the crisis. The desperation is full of pain and an agony that only the soul can know. The discomfort is painful because we don't know when the pain will stop. The heart aches, the soul throbs and the body is weary. Yet the desperate heart is willing to wait and be touched by the Comforter. The desperate heart can say even while the soul throbs in agony, "I will remain confident in this: I will see the goodness of the Lord in the land of the living" (Psalm 27:13, NIV). The desperate heart accepts God's timing for all things and not only waits but hopes in the Lord.

Obedience

How long had this man sat and waited? He waited every day. He waited for someone to help him with anything and everything. He could do nothing else but wait. Sometimes, your crisis demands for you to wait. My crisis seemed to command that I wait. Some days were so difficult. I wanted to see change. I also struggled with the temptation to make things change. Of course, I desired for my circumstances to change for the better. Wanting my circumstances to change was never the issue. I struggled with the temptation to manipulate the change so I could be comfortable. To take control of my circumstances would only give me temporary relief. Therein lies the great dilemma. We can either take control and manipulate our circumstances and experience temporary relief, or we can wait in the hope of Christ and have a life restored by his grace. To have the latter we must choose to obey the One who doesn't always relieve our pain but will always restore our hearts.

On the day Jesus stooped down in front of this blind man did he realize the waiting was over? Not only was the waiting over; life as he knew it would end.

Jesus sent this man to wash in the pool to test his obedience. This man lived in a time of religious legalism, ruled by pharisaical law. The religious rulers of that day took the law to a new level and developed a hardened heart that no one but God could break. Would this man be gripped by legalism or would he be changed by grace? This man wanted more than anything to see; he had desperate circumstances. This man also had a heart desperate to be made whole. He obeyed, washed in the pool, and came back seeing. Nothing mattered when Jesus asked him to do something that could have offended others. A heart that is desperate to be changed by Christ will obey with such great belief that people's opinions have no impact.

A Display of Grace

Before the healing, a question—maybe more like an accusation— was made about this man and his crisis of blindness. Jesus was asked who had sinned, the man or his parents, to cause the blindness. But Jesus did not get caught up in a ridiculous argument that would only bring more shame and not do any good. Jesus did not explain the reason but he did state the purpose, "'It was not that this man sinned, or his parents, but that the works of God might be displayed in him'" (John 9:3, ESV).

Our crisis is never about us. It is not for the purpose of keeping others' attention. You are noticed by others and I hope you are ministered to by others. I also hope that the ones who notice you and know you begin to ask questions. I also hope that their questions lead to answers about the Lord's purpose. Yes, we hurt, we ask all kinds of questions, we are discouraged, tired, empty, feel useless and want the crisis to be over and wish it had never come into our lives. Others will look at the life in crisis and ask some strange questions or even make accusations. During one particular season of my own crisis I was asked if I read my Bible anymore. I was told I needed to pray more. One person looked me directly in my eyes and asked if I was following the Lord. Those moments were painful, deeply painful. I wonder if the blind man heard the question that Jesus was asked and I wonder what he thought when Jesus answered. For each accusing question I was asked, there were also loving, godly people keeping me focused by reminding me God is good and that he knows all and sees all.

Nehemiah 2:18 states that they "strengthened their hands for the good work" (ESV). Friend, you may be the one in a crisis or you may be reading this so you can understand how to encourage the one you know whose life is changed by a crisis. There is work to do and it is a good work. The work is not to tire you or to keep you overwhelmed and in distress. The work to rebuild is for one purpose, "that the works of God might be displayed" in you (John 9:3, ESV).

Trust

The choice to rebuild your life after a crisis is an action of trust. Trusting the One who allowed the crisis to restore your life in his time will lead your desperate heart to follow him with an urgency that others will not understand. Nehemiah did not waste time in following the Lord's direction and he did not allow the discouragers to get in the way of his obedience. The blind man did not refuse God's healing that day when the method did not make sense. Jesus was asked what sin had caused this man to be blind but no one asked what the man did to cause the healing. It is easy to rationalize what could have caused your crisis but when God steps in and makes your life whole again it is difficult to deny God's amazing work and grace. Some will accept the work in your life amid your crisis and others will struggle. When God heals a life and makes one whole it may not make sense and it may not fit people's ideals.

How do you know if you are completely trusting God in your crisis? Trust can be measured by obedience. For the blind man, his obedience led to clarity. His inner sight was clear for his heart was pure. The healing power of Jesus had given him what he had never had: the ability to see. I don't know what you need to see and I don't know how you are struggling to trust God. I do know that the only way for any of us to have what we can't have apart from trusting the Lord is to obey and trust. When our Lord calls us to abide in him, to produce fruit, to have no bitterness, anger, idolatry, or sexual immorality then we have the choice. To trust, obey, and see clearly. When we choose to hold onto bitterness, anger, when we find comfort in our ideals, and when we try other things and relationships as the healer of our pain we get stuck and confused and we cannot see God.

God will bring healing and his timing will definitely be on time but his methods will never be what we think they should be. Some wouldn't accept the method, the day, or the person that healed the blind man. It didn't matter, because the blind man could see and that could not be denied.

Put your hands to the good work before you. The good work of rebuilding and restoring your life. Trust God to bring the necessary healing. His method to heal you will blow you away and the day he brings healing will be unexpected. The One who created time is not contained by time. The time to heal you belongs to him. Walk in obedience to his Word. Let others be amazed by the work of God displayed in your life. You were not created to stand in ruins and the stench of ashes. You were called to renewal and the sweet aroma of a life changed for his glory.

The word "blind" in John 9:1 can mean a physical or mental blindness. We know that the man in this passage was physically blind. However, I am encouraged to know that the Lord will bring clarity to my mind when it is blind. In a crisis, our mind can easily be blinded by the overwhelming emotions that the crisis causes. Obedience to the Lord is the only thing that will bring clarity to our mind and ease intense emotions that hurt us deeply.

God desires that through our obedience his work is displayed in our life. The things of the Lord will not only be made visible to us personally; others will see the Lord's work in our lives. When my oldest child was a toddler I began teaching her a simple phrase. It began with me saying to her, "We obey the first time with a happy attitude." Now that both my children are much older, I ask them, "When do we obey?" and they respond with "The first time." I ask, "With what?" and they answer, "A happy attitude." I have talked with them about the importance of this simple phrase that has complex implications. There will come a day that they will not answer to me anymore. For the rest of their lives they will answer to the Lord.

Attitude

A crisis changes our lives. Our reaction to the crisis changes our hearts. Our hearts can alter our view of eternity and our response to the Lord. If obedience leads to clarity then how are we to walk in obedience? God gives us instructions to follow. These instructions are for the purpose of testing the heart. Just as the patch over my son's eye was the practical instruction we were to follow, it was the frequent eye appointments that proved healing could only be measured by the physician's instruments. It is the same in our time of life-changing crisis. God has given practical instruction in his Word and it is only through abiding in him that he can measure our healing with his grace and mercy.

What are the daily instructions given to us? We find instructions in 1 Thessalonians 5:15–23: "See that no one repays anyone evil for evil, but always seek to do good to one another and to everyone. Rejoice always, pray without ceasing, give thanks in all circumstances; for this is the will of God in Christ Jesus for you. Do not quench the Spirit. Do not despise prophecies, but test everything; hold fast what is good. Abstain from every form of evil" (ESV).

The practicality of the Lord's instructions speaks directly to our attitude. Beginning with verse fifteen, "see that no one repays anyone evil for evil, but always seek to do good to one another and to everyone." Some circumstances within a crisis are personal because a person has caused the harm. This word "evil" means harm or bad things. We are told to not get even by doing harm to the person who has harmed us. It is tempting and at time justifiable why we should get even. However, the Lord gives opposing direction to this attitude. He tells us to always seek to do good to everyone. Why would he give us that particular command? Well, the word "seek" means to pursue. We need to be occupied with the pursuit of doing good. If we are intentional in pursuing good deeds toward others, we are less focused on doing harm. It is almost impossible to pursue good and seek revenge at the same time. Pursuing good will begin to shape your attitude into one that is open to receive healing. Plotting revenge and hoping to cause harm will only handicap the heart and harden one's soul, making it more difficult to be made whole.

Is it really possible to "rejoice always"? It is a choice to rejoice always. I know that in seeking to do good to others and for others there should be something to rejoice about. Maybe you find that it is difficult to be glad in your crisis. I know I did. What possibly could make me rejoice when my marriage was falling apart faster than I could catch the falling pieces? Then I realized that this instruction from God is not about saying that things or people make me rejoice. This word "rejoice" in this passage is an action verb. If I were to diagram the "rejoice always" then it would read: (you) rejoice always. My rejoicing is a choice. When our focus is on the Lord and the way he is leading and the steps he is taking to restore us, there will always be something to rejoice in. I rejoice in him!

I can rejoice in Christ as a result of my time in communion with him. "Pray without ceasing" is the instruction given. But is it realistic? I have learned that more often than not my prayer time is in my car, cooking dinner, folding laundry, when I run and walk for exercise, and in my quiet time with God. I am ready at all times to take everything to the Lord in prayer. I have realized that being in prayer challenges my attitude of self-reliance, of seeking justice on my own terms. It also grows the fruit of long-suffering. Prayer will give you the endurance needed to wait on the Lord. You will be focused on the Lord. As we abide in him and he abides with us, fruit grows out of the dry places that have been made by a crisis. Prayer is a way to experience rest from restless emotions because we are continuously coming to the Lord.

"Give thanks in all circumstances; for this is the will of God in Christ Jesus for you." I don't know how much clearer this instruction could be. Does the Lord really expect us to give thanks in all circumstances? Yes. It is only through giving thanks that we keep every door and window of our soul wide open to receive what the Lord has for us. I found that in giving thanks that I am able to see God in the details. I have never said "thank you" that I am divorced. However, I do give thanks for all the different ways the Lord provides for us, restores us, directs us, loves us, cleanses us, gives rest when we are weary, and on and on. When the crisis is so overwhelming and it is difficult to know how and why it happened, you have to look very hard at the minute details of the crisis. There you will find so much to give thanks for. It is God's will for us to give thanks. Often a crisis brings such confusion you are not sure what the Lord wants you to do. It is simple: he wants you to give thanks.

The next instruction intended to keep our attitude in check and motivate us to walk in obedience to the Lord is a challenging one. When my life seems unbalanced because of the unpredictable emotions and thoughts caused by my crisis, I battle with myself. The pity party is inviting and I want to give in and stay there. I feel justified in feeling sorry for myself or blaming others for the pain I am in. I also can enjoy hateful thoughts and bitterness that arise out of my crisis. It is me against the Holy Spirit. The Lord knows the battle. It is the reason we are called to die daily to ourselves. The instruction in 1 Thessalonians 5:19 is, "Do not quench the Spirit." This word "quench" means to extinguish or suppress. The only way to know that I am not quenching the Spirit is by what is seen in my life. Galatians 5:22 gives me what to measure as a result of choosing the opposite of quenching. I am to bear fruit of the Spirit: "love, joy, peace, patience, kindness, goodness, faithfulness, gentleness, and self-control" (ESV). When I give the Holy Spirit complete freedom to work in my life regardless of my circumstances, then I will bear his fruit. Your life may be cracked, dry, broken and unattractive but the Holy Spirit will grow beautiful fruit in those places. Others will see what is growing out of what is broken and be amazed.

Not only are we not to quench the Spirit; we are also told to "not despise prophecies, but test everything; hold fast to what is good." In simple terms we are not to dismiss those who speak into our lives when it comes to the purpose of our pain during our crisis. The Lord will give others insight for us and about us that we need to receive. As a part of listening to others, we also need to examine what they are telling us. The only way to truly know if what we are told is truth is through the Bible. There will be different people speaking to your situation but only the ones who stand on the authority of Scripture should be listened to. We are to take their words to us, filtered through Scripture, and find them useful to our circumstances.

For the one desiring to walk in obedience there is one more instruction to be carried out with wisdom. "Abstain from every form of evil." The word "form" can also mean "appearance." It is important for you and I living in the crisis to ask one type of question when faced with opportunity. What is the wisest thing for me to do? What is the wisest thing for me to say? What is the wisest response to have? Things that can cause more trouble can present as harmless. Taking the time to sort through what is being presented to you with wisdom and prayer can save a lot of heartache.

Trusting with an obedient heart will give you courage to follow the Lord's instructions. The instructions given end with the sweet purpose of the all-loving God: "Now may the God of peace himself sanctify you completely, and may your whole spirit and soul and body be kept blameless at the coming of our Lord Jesus Christ. He who calls you is faithful; he will surely do it" (1 Thessalonians 5:23–24, ESV). Our loving Heavenly Father wants to bring a quiet rest to our soul. He knows the struggle we have in our flesh, especially in time of deep hurt and unwanted pain. He knows the unrest we feel. He wants to meet you in your crisis. "Now may the God of peace himself sanctify you completely…" He is a personal God. Just like he walked the garden looking for Adam and Eve after they had sinned, he is coming to find you with a specific purpose. He desires to cleanse you and purify you. He wants to be right with you in the midst of all the heartache to purify you and set you apart, renewing your soul.

Results of Obedience and Trust

The blind man in John 9 was sent to wash in the Pool of Siloam which was just beyond the Fountain Gate. His need to have sight was great. His need to trust and obey was greater. Jesus gave him specific instructions to go to the pool and wash. This man made his way to the pool blind. I wonder if he doubted as he walked to the pool. Were there others leading him to the pool? Did they encourage him? I think this man went to the pool trusting that the man who sent him knew what he was doing. It is the same with us in our time of need. God's Word gives us instruction. He asks us to carry out those instructions trusting that there is a purpose and a plan to make us whole. If we don't walk in obedience we will never understand the purpose or see the plan come to completion. As you seek clarity in your crisis, understand that clarity can only come through trust and obedience. The latter part of 1 Thessalonians 5:23–24 states, "may your whole spirit and soul and body be kept blameless at the coming of our Lord Jesus Christ. He who calls you is faithful; he will surely do it."

The Lord wants to guard you in every area so that you will be blameless. In other words, he desires that no one criticize you. He wants us to conduct our lives in such a manner that all who watch us in our crisis will see the faithfulness of the Lord. "He who calls you is faithful; he will surely do it." He will protect you. He will sanctify you. He will be faithful to you. He will cover you with his grace and mercy. He will give sight to a heart blinded by the darkness of your crisis. He is only asking that you trust and obey Him.

CHAPTER NINE

Expectant Hope

Signs of Life

Living in a crisis creates expectancy. You think thoughts such as, *Maybe today will be better than yesterday* or *Maybe today I will receive the answers I need*. You hope today will provide something that will give you reason to keep moving forward, to continue to have hope. Hope. A sweet word to the one who longs to be whole, renewed, and restored. Hope is what keeps you looking ahead. Nehemiah went to Jerusalem with hope. The hope to rebuild what had been left in ruins and disgrace. Even after seeing the devastation, he had hope. Nehemiah 2:17–18 gives a glimpse of the hope Nehemiah had and gave to the people.

> Then I said to them, "You see the trouble we are in, how Jerusalem lies in ruins with its gates burned. Come, let us

build the wall of Jerusalem, that we may no longer suffer derision." And I told them of the hand of my God that had been upon me for good, and also of the words that the king had spoken to me. And they said, "Let us rise up and build." So they strengthened their hands for the good work (ESV).

To live in our crisis for God's works to be displayed, we cannot rebuild with a bumper sticker mentality. This is much deeper, vaster, and much more demanding than the sum of a few words. Hope is not a pep talk. Hope is not positive thoughts. Hope is not a pep rally, the victory chant before a game. Hope is Jesus! Hope is in Jesus, by Jesus, and through Jesus.

As I was finishing up the final corrections and tweaking parts of this manuscript, we had a tornado come through our area. As my children and I sat in the hallway under our staircase, I could hear and see the weather reports on the television. I hate tornadoes! I hate them so much I have never seen the Wizard of Oz beyond the part with the tornado. Weird, I know. Needless to say, I was very anxious. Suddenly there was a change in the wind, rain and the way the trees were blowing. I said with great urgency to my children, "Get in the closet!" We moved quickly into the closet and waited. The power went out and then I heard a snap. We waited a total of about twenty minutes and the wind died down and the rain became normal. It was coming down horizontally, no longer coming down in all directions. My son said in an excited voice, "Mom, a tree is on our house!" There it was, a good-sized tree completely blocking our front porch. It had hit the roof above the porch. Thankfully there was no major damage to our home.

As we have waited for our power to come back on, to have water, and begin cleaning up the debris, I have thought about those few minutes in the closet. For some of you, your crisis has been the tornado of a lifetime. It came up suddenly, wreaked havoc, moved on and left a big mess for you to clean up. Our weekend will be spent picking up the mess. I still cannot get away from how the time in the closet affected my perception and perspective. In fact, as I write this, we are staying with friends because it could be several days before we have power.

The closet gave me hope that we were safe. We had taken all the precautions we could. As we waited in the closet I peeked out to look outside the window not far from the closet door. I was nervous and scared. However, being in the closet brought solace to the threat of what could be and what was happening all around us.

This is what it is to hope. We are in Christ. I couldn't stop that tornado. I couldn't get out of the path of the tornado. I couldn't stop the tree from falling. All I could do is get in the closet and wait. Dear one, you can't stop a crisis. You can't arrange your life in such a way to avoid a crisis. You are a crisis magnet because you are alive. Jesus said in John 16:33, "In the world you will have tribulation" (ESV). This is not a maybe. This is a fact. I guess I will never understand why we seem to be surprised when trouble comes. I get frustrated when trouble comes and sometimes I do respond in surprise.

When the local weather emergency center said that anyone in our area was to immediately get in a closet or a basement, it was not a suggestion. It was a command. Getting in something that would hold was the only way to handle the storm headed our way. It is only "in Christ" that we can be saved. In Christ, we will never thirst again (John 6:35). In Christ, we will not remain in darkness

(John 12:46). In Christ, we will live even after we die (John 11:25). In Christ, we have peace (John 16:33).

If I can say one thing to you that will make the difference in moving you from crisis to credibility, it is to be in Christ! Romans 5:1–5 reminds us:

> Therefore, since we have been justified by faith, we have peace with God through our Lord Jesus Christ. Through him we have also obtained access by faith into this grace in which we stand, and we rejoice in hope of the glory of God. Not only that, but we rejoice in our sufferings, knowing that suffering produces endurance, and endurance produces character, and character produces hope, and hope does not put us to shame, because God's love has been poured into our hearts through the Holy Spirit who has been given to us (ESV).

The particular phrase in these verses, "Through him we have also obtained access by faith into this grace in which we stand..." caught my attention. The New American Standard Bible translation reads, "through whom also we have obtained our introduction by faith into this grace in which we stand."

We are loved by a kind God. He is holy, just, and righteous. He is jealous for us. He is willing to do whatever it takes to introduce us to grace. The only way for us to know grace is through faith. I know when I was in the early days of my crisis I wanted someone to lead me to someone with answers. I called close friends who knew of biblically grounded counselors. Maybe you find yourself doing the same thing. You desire to meet others who have experienced what you are experiencing. When those times happen you are grateful to the person who introduced you to someone who truly understands all that you are going through.

In this particular verse in Romans that is the picture painted: an introduction by one who knows someone. In this case it is faith that has the ability to introduce us to grace. In the beginning of your crisis you might have held tight to your faith. Maybe you did not have faith in the beginning and now you are realizing that faith is a necessity. It is never too late. I discovered that adding and listening to new worship songs to my playlist helped immensely. Songs about faith in the Lord consoles the hurting heart. Writing Bible verses on note cards is a wonderful way to keep your thoughts fixed on his Word. Your faith digs deep and you hope the faith you have is strong, because you are weak.

The shift of a crisis will create opportunity for grace. This is a two-fold experience. First, we are not born into this world knowing grace. Grace has to be received through Jesus Christ. Scripture tells us, "For by grace you have been saved through faith. And this is not your own doing; it is the gift of God, not a result of works, so that no one may boast" (Ephesians 2:8–9, ESV). At salvation it is faith that introduces us to faith. As a follower of Jesus living in crisis mode, it will be your faith that brings you to his sufficient grace (2 Corinthians 12:9). Second, you and I could be similar in that we were following Christ before the crisis turned our lives upside down. Our opportunity for grace is the kind that introduces us to the all-sufficient Heavenly Father.

Times of Trouble

Trouble is coming. Being "in Christ" is not a suggestion. I was not happy about the tornado but I sure was glad about the closet under our stairwell. Paul, the writer of Romans, knew trouble is part of living. Yet, he stated that we can rejoice in our trouble, "knowing that suffering produces endurance." You may be thinking like me: *How in the world can I rejoice in what I am going through?* You can when you know *Who* you are in. Being in Christ gives perspective. It is stated in these verses. We can know that the crisis we face will produce continuous patience. In other words, you can accept the waiting. This waiting will bring forth a proven worth. How many times when a crisis has blown into your life have you thought (or someone may have said to you) that it will be worth it one day, and you will understand more as time goes on. Don't you just want to know if all this trouble is worth it? The trouble is not worth it. You are worth it. The trouble is there to produce in you and for you something greater: your relationship in Christ.

What does it look like to rejoice in our suffering? The outcome of suffering is priceless when you have insight into and purpose for the suffering. The fruit that will grow when we endure suffering is what the heart must have to be made whole. As a counselor, I delight when those seeking help are willing to take the small steps that will lead to leaps of intentional living. In so doing they find the life they have longed for, a life free from the grip of bitterness and anger that can easily be nurtured because of the crisis.

Many times we can be so focused on the turmoil that trouble brings that we neglect to step back and see the bigger picture. There is a personal invitation that trouble sends. The invitation is for our character. Maybe we need to be more controlled and less controlling. Perhaps our personality is unbridled. An unbridled personality is a dangerous personality. Thoughts that run rampant with anxiety, what-ifs, anger, and bitter responses will handicap you. I find it interesting that the only way for some things to be completely changed is through the fire of suffering.

Our character is an area that can be settled into old ways and problematic responses. It is no mistake that the Lord states in Romans 5, "endurance produces character." Endurance will prove your character. Only a proven character can be proven through the Lord. In essence, a proven character is one that has submitted to the authority of Jesus Christ.

Paul writes in Romans that character produces hope. Pay attention to the steps! It is important that we get this. Faith introduces us to grace. Through this we can rejoice in our suffering because it is suffering that produces endurance (stamina). This stamina will manufacture character (moral fiber). If you desire to thrive in the midst of your crisis, you need moral fiber. This will slam your soul into a head on collision with hope. The kind of hope that will not disappoint, bring shame, or humiliation.

The Love of God

And then hope is the end result of one who chooses to rejoice in the crisis. As Nehemiah said, the joy of the Lord is my strength (Nehemiah 8:10). When you read this passage you can sense the building of excitement as if the writer is saying, "Wait for it… wait for it." Then God promises "hope will not disappoint," it is a guarantee. I am so glad that hope will not disappoint, because life lived in crisis is full of disappointment. In fact, a crisis guarantees disappointments. Not hope! How? The answer, in Romans 5:5, is five words long and the sweetest words in Scripture: "because the love of God" (NASB).

He doesn't love you just when crisis comes; he pours it out all over you all the time. As you end the day, you may dread facing more of the same turmoil and pain tomorrow. I remember those days. Every once in a while I have a day like that. I am so grateful that those days are fewer and farther between. The wounds of my crisis are still healing and I am putting my hands to the good work of rebuilding. Get in Christ. He is your hope and healer. He is your protector. He is your light in darkness. He sustains you. He gives your rest. He makes all things new.

CHAPTER TEN

Digging Deep

The Well of Joy

Near the beginning of my separation from my husband I heard the most encouraging sermon. I needed to hear the words of truth. I downloaded the sermon and have listened to it so often that I have almost memorized it word for word. Every time I listen to the pastor preach his sermon entitled "He is in your Storm," I never tire of hearing one particular statement. Pastor Johnny Hunt says, "Sometimes God chooses to dig the well of joy with the spade of sorrow." Read that statement again and let it settle in your heart. The first time I heard that statement, I purposed in my heart that no matter what may come I would be all right with God digging into my life, unearthing everything dear to me. I trusted that one day what had been an ugly hole in my life with no obvious usefulness would one day become a well of joy and everyone would know God is here.

When God chooses to dig in and dig up your life, there is fear. In Nehemiah's account of the fifty-two day rebuilding of his beloved city, we are introduced to people who made it their purpose to mock, distract, and discourage (Nehemiah 2). One particular individual is described as grieved, angry, mocking, and distracting. Unfortunately as you rebuild from your crisis there will be others who desire to sabotage your efforts. Sadly, there could be Christians who will have these same attitudes toward you. Press on! Put your hands to the work of rebuilding and do not be distracted from following the steps the Lord has directed for you to take.

In Nehemiah 4 the people of Jerusalem are described as having a mind to work. The people had a determination of will to get to work and stay to see the job completed. This was far more than a decision to get the job done; this was an emotional decision. They were passionate about what they were doing. Sanballat and Tobiah wanted to do more than mock and discourage Nehemiah and the people from rebuilding. Their desire and plan was to hinder the work of rebuilding.

No matter what or how they tried to distract Nehemiah, he would not leave the good work. No matter what pulls you or who tempts you with distraction or mocks your progress, stay the course. Staying the course is difficult. There may be times that you want to confront your accusers, the ones who mock you and want to hinder the restoration process, with explanation and defense of the work you are doing. Your crisis may be one where others are extremely sympathetic but think you are too fragile and cannot move forward. Whatever is vying for your attention and pulling you away from the task of rebuilding, remain faithful to the calling of restoration.

Priorities

Worship God daily with your actions, attitude, and thoughts. Continuously remind yourself that restoration begins through worship. Others may not be able to understand why you are rebuilding the way you are and you yourself may not be able to see how it will all come together. Obedience will lead to clarity. Obeying God's Word is the most effective thing for the rebuilding of your life. If you are in God's Word and applying his principles to the task of rebuilding, not only will you be effective but you will be infectious. God's work in your life will be on display in such a way that it will inspire all those watching.

Living a life ruined as a result of a crisis is no excuse to live impurely. In fact, the crisis that has brought ruin and has changed your life should be a motivator to live purely before the Lord and become as spiritually healthy as you can. The continuous removal of bitterness, anger, and undisciplined ways is imperative to living a blameless life before the Lord. Warning to those of us that pursue a life of purity: we will be faced with loneliness. That loneliness can and will distract you and tempt you to avoid that awful feeling. Philippians 4:8 helps us know what is pure and what is not. This verse is speaking directly to our thought life. However, if you and I can remain keenly aware of our thoughts and stop things there then our actions will remain pure. This verse states, "Finally, brothers, whatever is true, whatever is honorable, whatever is just, whatever is pure, whatever is lovely, whatever is commendable, if there is any excellence, if there is anything worthy of praise, think about these things" (ESV). Actions follow thoughts. You may want to numb the loneliness with fleeting pleasures. There is hard work to do in the restoration process and giving into the temptation to deal with your loneliness in unhealthy ways will only lead to greater grief and more exaggerated regret.

Peace Will Guard You

The valley that is created by a crisis is treacherous. The fear of the unknown and the shock left behind once the crisis hit is too much to bear. When David penned the words, "through the valley of the shadow of death," the death is so final. A crisis can bring about more than one type of death. Because of that we can easily obsess over the many things we have lost. So much loss, so much pain, and so much sadness will break anyone. But you are anchored by the One who will never leave you, never disappoint you, and never let you go. He can give you peace when there are so many things you do not and may never understand.

Allowing the peace of God to guard your heart will produce amazing results. You will need your heart guarded as you rebuild. The heart is easily swayed. Many will give you good advice and have good intentions for what they think you should do. Only time spent in prayer seeking God's plan for your rebuilding will result in great things. Don't let the good things get in the way of the great things. Be very intentional in your prayer time and studying God's Word. He is the gatekeeper of your soul and he has the ultimate authority over what comes in to your life. A heart guarded by the authority of Jesus Christ will lead to a life completely surrendered to His plan of restoration. The heart that is guarded with the peace of God will live with the expectant hope that tomorrow is settled because the all-present God is already there.

Courage

No matter your reason for being examined, have the courage to walk in his light and let the light of God's truth reveal your heart, thoughts, motives, and actions. Respond to sin with a godly sorrow and respond to false accusations with humility. As you rebuild this may be the most difficult part of the process. Be of good courage.

Resolve to serve the Lord. Trust that as he digs deeper that joy is coming. You will be able to say as Job did, "I will come out as gold" (Job 23:10, ESV). Our Lord judges with kindness and wisdom. Trust his judgment in your life knowing that his desire is to present you blameless.

A day will come, if it hasn't already, when you will begin to share the goodness of the Lord. You will share his truths that never change. You will find that the story of your crisis is never about what happened but what God did. You will get to tell others the great things that have been accomplished because God rebuilt your life. The details of your crisis will fade into the light of his glory and his sovereign love. Others will only see the compassion of the Heavenly Father on an undeserving life. They will hunger to know the One who restores ruins, makes something whole from brokenness, and turns shame to a shining light of hope. You will not be known as the person to whom something bad happened; instead you will be known as the person God changed.

Your crisis and my crisis is our opportunity for joy. The gaping hole that crisis creates is the perfect place for God to spring up a well that will bring forth a legacy of joy. Dare to consider giving God complete freedom to dig deep into your life. Can you envision the well of joy that can replace the hole of despair and disgrace? Your crisis does not mean your life is over. Your crisis is the call to opportunity. Are you ready to let God dig? Are you ready to obey his leading and put your hands to this good work? Are you ready to take the opportunity that God is offering to you through heartache, tears, and pain? An opportunity for joy doesn't come through good times and pleasantries. This kind of opportunity is a personal invitation from the almighty God to you asking you to put your hope in him. That hope will not disappoint.

Joy

During the summer of 2012 my daughter had hit her breaking point with her Movement Disorder. In early 2009, she was diagnosed with Dystonia. We have a wonderful doctor and he was able to diagnose her and put her on the medication that her body will respond to. Needless to say, medicine helps but does not cure. She has more good days than bad days. With the constant movement of her muscles which are allowed some but not full relief, she tires easily and is often sore. For a few weeks she would cry. She would tell me that she just wanted to be normal. She expressed through tears that she wanted to go one day with no movements. I would encourage her and pray with and for her. I would hold her and cry with her. I would pray to the Lord the type of prayers that only my mother's heart could utter. However, I knew the Lord was leading me to be quiet with my responses to her. I struggled with this. If you are a mother, you know that it is difficult for a mama to keep her mouth shut when it comes to her kids. However, the Lord was making it clear to me to remain quiet, and I did.

One day my daughter unexpectedly came down the stairs calling to me. With uncontainable excitement she declared, "I know why I have a movement disorder!" What came out of her mouth next I did not expect and it brought me to tears. She said with a smile, "It is my opportunity for joy." I hugged her tightly and while holding her I knew why I was to be silent. The Lord needed me to be quiet so he could dig deep into her soul. In other words, I had to get out of the way. He wanted to dig and he needed time alone with her to dig. On that day, standing in the kitchen, my daughter knew her spade of sorrow had dug a well of joy.

The challenging part of stepping aside and letting God dig as deep as he needs to and for as long as he deems best is the "stepping aside" part. You may recognize it better in Paul's words written in

Galatians 2:20: "I have been crucified with Christ. It is no longer I who live, but Christ who lives in me. And the life I now live in the flesh I live by faith in the Son of God, who loved me and gave himself for me" (ESV).

Get Out Of The Way

The only way for Christ to have complete freedom to work in our lives and restore the ruins of a crisis is when we are crucified with Christ. This word "crucify" is a verb. It requires daily action on our behalf. Christ died by way of crucifixion and we are to die to ourselves daily. I choose not to be the supervisor in the digging process. By dying daily to my wants, my desires, and my way of doing things I become a willing participant who is shaped and changed, and who accepts the pain that is part of the process. In dying to self, I become identified with Christ. Dying to self is acknowledging and then denying the things that are led by my flesh. It could be practical, daily things, deeper emotional reactions, the way you think toward others, or an attitude toward spiritual matters. A daily habit that I had for several years was drinking a particular brand of diet soda. I realized that my craving for this was not good for me physically. With the help of the Lord, I stopped drinking diet soda months ago. The Lord began to convict me in how I respond when I am running behind schedule. Instead of barking commands at my children for them to hurry up, I had to die to my way of motivating them. I have not perfected this but I am so thankful that I much more gentle in how I communicate time to them. I am more tender and they are more relaxed. Dying to self is individualized. What I need to die to is different from what you need to die to. It can range from practical things that the Lord wants to work in you for the sake of discipline, to deeper issues that address and change your character. Whatever it is, I trust that you will be willing to die so that you can really live.

"It is no longer I who live, but Christ who lives in me." Identifying with Christ is the way we are choosing to live. "I" have been put to death. Christ lives in me. This is where you will begin to know the joy of the Lord. You will understand how you rejoice in your suffering. You will become credible regardless of the crisis. All of this is because Christ lives in you. He is the credible one and His life fully living in you is the only way to be credible. You no longer rebuild your life on opinions. You rebuild on the principles and promises of the One who gives eternal life. In being identified with Christ, your focus shifts from earthly concerns to eternal perspective. Everything we do in our crisis and during our crisis can be accomplished with an eternal perspective. It is this perspective that will change everything. An eternal perspective is in the details. It is dying daily, identifying with Christ every day, and being aware of all the ways Christ will live in you.

"And the life I now live in the flesh I live by faith in the Son of God." This life we live is finite and fragile. Some of us live in the fragile places every day. We know all too well that fragile things break. We live in the broken place. I am emotional as I write this because I will never comprehend the love that is God. He stands in the broken places with us. We can live, thriving and confident, because "I live by faith in the Son of God." A crucified life in Christ can only live by faith in Christ. Everything is through him. As we rebuild and are restored, we must never take for granted the One who gave the strength, the insight, the wisdom, the provisions, the direction, the loving people in our time of greatest need, the grace, the mercy, the stamina, and the overwhelming love. It is by faith that I can live with the reminders of my crisis because the Son of God is the only one who can make something beautiful from ashes. He is the only one who can pick up a spade made of deep sorrow and use that same sorrow to dig a deep well that will only bring forth joy. Dear one, this is the kind of faith to live by!

Dig Deeper

The One who will dig deep is the same One who gave himself for you. His great love for us can never be comprehended. The Old Testament prophet Isaiah wrote of the Messiah who would come. Jesus did come and he does understand our sorrow.

> He was despised and rejected by men; a man of sorrows, and acquainted with grief; and as one from whom men hide their faces he was despised, and we esteemed him not. Surely he has borne our grief and carried our sorrows; yet we esteemed him stricken, smitten by God, and afflicted. But he was pierced for our transgressions; he was crushed for our iniquities; upon him was the chastisement that brought us peace, and with his wounds we are healed (Isaiah 53: 3–5, ESV).

Do you want to see the well of joy bubbling up? In my mind, I picture a stone well surrounded with a beautiful landscape of colorful flowers that will catch the attention of others as they watch my life. This is what I desire for others to see. Instead of seeing the mess that comes with rebuilding, the untidy places that for a time have been left because more important matters demand attention, or the areas that need more detailed work, I want everyone to see the well. If others can see the well then I know they are seeing Jesus right there in the middle of my mess. I desire to know intimately "the man of sorrows," the One "acquainted with grief." Don't you think if the man of sorrows who is acquainted with grief is digging your well of joy, he truly understands every tear that falls and sees every time you wince in pain? "He was despised and rejected by men." Jesus, the son of God, the only begotten son, and the One who came to seek and save the lost was considered worthless and rejected by men. Friend, the methods he may use to dig your well of joy may not always make sense but please don't think they are worthless or think Christ is worthless. Don't reject the One who gives meaning to the pain. He is the only one who can take what we deem worthless and make it worthy in Himself.

Christ came to bring truth. He tells us in John 14:6 that he is "'the way, and the truth, and the life. No one comes to the Father except through me'" (ESV). Please don't enter into the greatest crisis the soul can experience by rejecting the truth of Christ. Rejecting His way will create chaos of the soul.

He came as our Savior to endure our grief and carry our sorrows. He did not stop there, though. He was wounded for our sins. He was broken for our depravity. He took the discipline that we should be receiving. By his wounds we are completely healed. Don't dismiss the One who will dig the well of joy in the middle of all the mess that He has already endured.

Dear one, God has his spade and he is offering you one also. Hold your spade and grip it with all your might and then dig, baby, dig! Dig, build, remove rubble, cry, hurt, rejoice, worship, and dig deeper. As you strengthen your hands to the good work you will find that the joy of the Lord is your strength. What an opportunity you have right in the middle of the most devastating time of your life. What will you do with the opportunity for joy?

I am so thankful that I made the choices to dig deeper. I am seeing the small signs of bubbling joy begin to fill my well. I am blessed to be a part of a church family that pours love over us on a regular basis. More importantly, my children have godly men in their life who spend time with them. The pastor of our church includes my son on hunting trips and spends time talking with him about biblical masculinity. It is so helpful to have that kind of influence in my son's life. My daughter experiences healthy relationships with godly men as well. One of my favorite things to watch is her talking with our pastor. He gives her his undivided attention. On hot, summer days those interactions may include the two of them eating ice cream together. He invests in her spiritually and walks her through Bible verses. He and his wife have told me on several occasions that they love my children as if they were their own. I believe that because of how they invest in my children's lives.

As for me, personally, I know this well is bubbling with joy because of the healing that has taken place in my heart and mind. I know my scars are a part of me and I am able to see them not as scars of pain but marks of grace. I laugh a lot. I have a deep, abiding joy. The Lord has placed in my life some of the sweetest and funniest friends since our most recent move. Laughter is medicine to the heart (Prov. 17:22)! As I write, I listen to the bubbling creek outside my window and am reminded that God restores. He does turn your mourning into joy (Psalm 30:11). Our family is rich in his mercy. I desire for us to give richly to others as well. The song "God of My days" has become somewhat of anthem for our family. Sung by Gateway Worship and written by Zach Neese, the lyrics are powerful and help me and my children apply an eternal perspective to our pain. The words to the chorus are:

> You're the God of my days, the King of my nights
> Lord of my laughter, sovereign in sorrow
> You're the Prince of my praise, the love of my life
> You never leave me, You are faithful, God of my days

Dear one, when you begin to live only for Christ in your crisis, the well is dug deeper and the joy overflows and overflows. I have no regrets that I surrendered to my Heavenly Father and the spade he used to dig the well of joy in my life. The crisis devastated me and I will feel its effects the rest of my life. But his grace and mercy overshadow my crisis. I am not defined by my crisis even though I could easily be labeled. I no longer have an identity crisis because I am in him. We can know that our lives can move from crisis to credibility because we can choose to be crucified with Christ and live the restored life saying, "nevertheless I live; yet not I, but Christ lives in me: and the life which I now live in the flesh I live by the faith of the Son of God, who loved me, and gave himself for me."

CHAPTER ELEVEN

Crisis to Credibility

A Contagious Faith

I still remember the evening I showed my mom the spots on my legs and she told me I had the chicken pox. My entire second grade class came down with the virus. I am sure our teacher was thrilled to have an unexpected break. I can remember, as the first few children were showing symptoms, overhearing one mother say she intentionally sent her child to visit another who had the chicken pox. Back then, the chicken pox was like a rite of passage. I still find it interesting that the one mother wanted her child to be with the child who was contagious. The only way to get the chicken pox was to be exposed to the virus. Our second grade classroom was a petri dish ready to expose an infectious virus.

I have walked in my crisis—separation and divorce—during the last five years and now share the valuable treasures the Lord has given to me. I want to share one last thought with you. Not only do I hope you will do the hard work of rebuilding; I also hope you will be contagious. I desire for you to place your trust in the One who will restore you. I want more than anything for you to rebuild in such a way that you never be non communicable during your crisis or after it is over. The contagious person is the authentic individual who understands what real exposure is like and why it is needed. I am not talking about being exposed as we have unpacked in earlier chapters. I am speaking to the type of exposure where others want to be with you and near you. Your deep, abiding faith in Christ infects their soul.

I know in today's culture we hear the word authentic a lot. In fact, it probably is overused. However, it's the term that exactly fits. Just as Nehemiah and the people of Jerusalem hung the gates and locked the doors, you and I have one last gate to build, hang, and lock. This gate is the gate that speaks of your life. All who enter into your life through this gate will be exposed.

As I Am

The "A" in authentic is understanding God loves me "As I Am." I can say with confidence I AM (one of my favorite names for God) loves me as I am. I cannot present myself clean enough, good enough, or appealing enough. I am a sinner, regardless of the crisis I am living in or all the reasons why my crisis has happened. Romans 3:23 states that "for all have sinned and fall short of the glory of God" (ESV). We fail. Our sin, which we are born with, keeps us from God. He cannot be near sin. He is holy. Before you lose hope and label yourself a failure, remember that God has a plan of redemption through his son Jesus. Through Jesus' death and resurrection, he is the way to God the Father. Paul stated clearly in his letter to the Colossians,

> He is the image of the invisible God, the firstborn of all creation. For by him all things were created, in heaven and on earth, visible and invisible, whether thrones or dominions or rulers or authorities—all things were created through him and for him. And he is before all things, and in him all things hold together. And he is the head of the body, the church. He is the beginning, the firstborn from the dead, that in everything he might be preeminent. For in him all the fullness of God was pleased to dwell, and through him to reconcile to himself all things, whether on earth or in heaven, making peace by the blood of his cross. And you, who once were alienated and hostile in mind, doing evil deeds, he has now reconciled in his body of flesh by his death, in order to present you holy and blameless and above reproach before him (Col. 1:15–22, ESV).

Did you catch it? At the end of the passage: "…[Jesus] has now reconciled in his body of flesh by his death, in order to present you holy and blameless and above reproach before him." The letter A that stands for "As I Am" is so much more than you realize! Jesus does present you as you are before God. We can rest in knowing that even in our crisis we don't have to present our case, our wounds, or our brokenness. We can stand confidently as we are, knowing that Jesus Christ presents us. We will be "As I Am" covered in his blood standing assured that the Almighty God, creator of Heaven and Earth sees us holy and blameless and above reproach.

Understanding God's Plan

Many times I have read Jeremiah 29:11–13 and wondered how this piece of the puzzle fits. "For I know the plans I have for you, declares the LORD, plans for welfare and not for evil, to give you a future and a hope. Then you will call upon me and come and pray to me, and I will hear you. You will seek me and find me, when you seek me with all your heart" (ESV). The word "plans" means "thoughts." God thinks thoughts toward us that are wonderful and full of promise. These thoughts are of us being complete, peaceful, and favorable. He does not have thoughts of distress or misery. He desires to give us a future and an expectation that can only be found in him. He will hear our call. He will hear us when we cry out to him.

How often have you been in a situation with several small children? One will cry, and immediately the parents know it is their child. The other parents take notice but they do not move toward that child with urgency. Why? It is not their child. A loving parent knows his or her child. If you are following Christ then God is your Heavenly Father and he does hear his child cry out. He hears with discernment. It does not take long for parents to recognize the unique meanings of their child's different cries. When the child is yours, you become discerning. God knows us better that we know ourselves and he can discern our heart's cry. How can we begin to understand God's plan for us when everything about our crisis is difficult to make sense of? We seek. We search. We do those two things with all of our heart. We never let up. As we seek and as we search, we may not find all of the answers we *think* we need. But we find the One we need. We find God.

Total Surrender

Surrender is a word that is often said but most difficult to act on. The definition of surrender is to yield to the possession or power of another. The power of a crisis is overpowering and we can easily surrender to the demise of the crisis. God has a different plan: the process of surrendering to him and his power. All of us second graders infecting one another with the chicken pox virus could only happen when we surrendered to the power of the virus. Our immune symptoms had to completely yield to the power of the virus. Similarly, being in the Word of God daily gives us the courage to surrender. 2 Timothy 3:16–17 explains to us the purpose of God's Word in our life: "All Scripture is breathed out by God and profitable for teaching, for reproof, for correction, and for training in righteousness, that the man of God may be complete, equipped for every good work" (ESV). Only the courageous choose surrender. The bravest thing we can do is surrender to the Almighty God. Some will watch your life in crisis and compliment your bravery or comment on how well you are handling things. I would hear things like that and wonder what they would think if they knew how fearful I was. Most of my journal entries in 2008 were on surrender. I purposed in my heart to surrender to the process of the reproof, the correction, the training in righteousness, and the teaching of God's Word. Surrender to the all-powerful God is the only way I get the strength I need for the restoration process. If we truly desire to be "complete, equipped for every good work," then our only option is to surrender to the Lord.

Just as Nehemiah encouraged the people to put their hands to the good work, we too can do the same thing. Surrendering to the process of rebuilding is difficult at times. Walking in obedience to the Lord is the greatest act of surrender. We surrender our way of doing things, our attitudes of bitterness and resentment. We surrender our anger and our anxiety. One of the most difficult things I had to surrender was my way of pleading with my then husband. I realized that the years of pleading with him had become about me being comfortable and wanting to know I was loved. Fear motivated my pleading. The day came that I was faced with the opportunity to surrender my fear. I had always had the opportunity but this particular time was different because my pain had now become greater than my fear. To surrender my fear meant I had to surrender, to let go of my old ways of soothing my fears. I had to stop pleading. I had to stop asking for him to love me. I had to stop pushing him to seek out others who could help. I had to surrender like this on a daily basis. My faith in the Lord fought a fierce battle with the fear that gripped my heart. What I feared most was what the Lord was calling me to surrender: the outcome. People usually fall into either the fight or flight category of response. I am a fighter, and since I was fighting for my marriage I was willing to do whatever it took to save it. Yet as I fought I realized I was only willing to surrender what I was comfortable with. What the Lord was calling me to do made me afraid because I did not know what it would look like. I knew I wasn't to give up on my relationship with my husband. I realized as the days and months turned into years that the Lord was showing me how shallow I was in my surrender. It is easy to say that God is good when he answers prayers the way we want, when he brings much needed relief from pain, or when he unexpectedly blesses us. What he wanted me to understand and experience is that he is good even when he answers prayers not to my liking, when he chooses not to bring relief the way I prefer, or when there are no obvious signs of blessing. He wanted me to surrender that outcome, with a deep understanding that he is good. What he did or didn't do would not make him more or less good. Whether my marriage was restored or whether I was abandoned, he is good. When I surrendered my fear and was no longer overpowered by it, faith took over and sweet rest entered my soul. Surrendering to the process of letting the Lord work in my circumstances was the only way for the truth of my situation to be revealed.

Honesty

To be authentic people who are being restored to credibility, we must be honest. If we desire to be contagious, then we must live a life of confession, keeping our hearts continuously open to the quickening of the Holy Spirit. If we hide our sin then our life will never be infectious for the Gospel. Proverbs 28:13 states clearly, "Whoever conceals his transgressions will not prosper, but he who confesses and forsakes them will obtain mercy" (ESV). Confession goes hand in hand with forsaking. We confess and we abandon the sin that has entangled us. We make deliberate choices to never be entangled by that sin again. We can live in the messy rebuilding of our crisis, and obtain mercy. What others will begin to see in our life is the tender affection poured over us by a loving God.

As we confess our sins to the Lord and abandon those sins in our life, we also are to confess our sins to others. "Therefore, confess your sins to one another and pray for one another, that you may be healed. The prayer of a righteous person has great power as it is working" (James 5:16b, ESV). I have already mentioned the five women who continually walked with me through my crisis. Some might label them as my accountability partners. They serve an important role as I confess to them my struggles, my temptations, and my sin. The times I have confessed something personal to them has been some of the sweetest times because they have prayed with me and for me. My humbling myself and being vulnerable gave them specific direction in how to pray for me. When we are honest about our condition, particularly the condition of our heart we become contagious. It is humility that begins to grow the first signs of an infectious faith. God gives one of the most powerful and sweetest promises in 1 John 1:9: "If we confess our sins, he is faithful and just to forgive us our sins and to cleanse us from all unrighteousness." Our requirement is to confess. His promise is to be faithful, forgive, and cleanse. To have my sin forgiven and my wounds cleansed is so appealing to me. Open wounds become infected. Wounds cleansed with the salve of his righteousness heal and become beautiful scars.

Executing God's Plan

As we look for opportunities to carry out God's plan we will discover moments of inexplicable joy. Dear friend, God has not brought you this far and given you the strength to rebuild only to have you keep it to yourself. He will bring people to you, and give you opportunities to speak up and show compassion for others wounded by their own crises. The plan is to share the hope and the truth of Jesus Christ. "How beautiful upon the mountains are the feet of him who brings good news, who publishes peace, who brings good news of happiness, who publishes salvation, who says to Zion, 'Your God reigns'"(Isaiah 52:7, ESV). You will be most beautiful when you are the messenger of peace and happiness. You will be able to say with confidence that "your God reigns." What a testimony that the One for whom you live can use your mess as his message.

The writer of Proverbs gives us a glimpse what it is like for the person to whom you minister when you are open to sharing your story. What does it mean to know that what God has done in your life—even as it fell apart—will refresh someone else's life? "The light of the eyes rejoices the heart, and good news refreshes the bones" (Proverbs 15:30, ESV). What if you are like cold water to a thirsty soul? "Like cold water to a thirsty soul, so is good news from a far country" (Proverbs 25:25, ESV). I have never met anyone who would refuse rejuvenated water to quench their thirst. Don't cower in fear that others would not want to hear the hope you have to tell about. Don't be lulled into complacency if your crisis is over, thinking no one would be interested. Those of us who are wounded, broken, and beautifully scarred by a crisis have a responsibility to the One who has made us credible.

No Comparing

Our crisis is not for the purpose of comparing to what someone else has endured. Comparing will lead to carelessness. When we become careless we then will neglect the important things. Important things aren't things at all. What is most important are the people God has placed in our sphere of influence. If we begin to compare our crisis to someone else's crisis then we lose perspective and purpose. The challenge of the authentic person who is thriving in a crisis is summed up in 1 Timothy 6:6: "But godliness with contentment is great gain" (ESV). Another translation reads, "But godliness *actually* is a means of great gain when accompanied by contentment" (ESV). In other words, the godly person living in a crisis has a greater ability to affect others when he or she is also content. Take to heart what Paul wrote: "For the sake of Christ, then, I am content with weaknesses, insults, hardships, persecutions, and calamities. For when I am weak, then I am strong" (2 Corinthians 12:10, ESV). Paul wrote this after he had revealed a thorn and had pleaded with the Lord three times to remove it. Scholars have different ideas about what this "thorn" was and what Paul meant by it. Some conclude that this thorn was not a literal thorn but a metaphor for some struggle. There is no way to know. However, Paul realized—just as you and I need to—that our circumstances may not change as we would prefer. Our crisis may last longer than we ever imagined. Regardless of my circumstances or my preferences, I have learned to trust the Lord. I want those standing over my grave to be able to say of me,

"There is a gal who pursued godliness wrapped in contentment and has been presented by Jesus Christ completely restored."

Can you live your life in crisis mode with contentment despite the details of your crisis? I hope that you allow the challenge of choosing contentment to build you up as an authentic follower of Christ. This strength that you will know is the strength of your soul. It is the power of the unlimited God that will carry you. This power is unleashed with more grace and greater force when you choose contentment.

Total Pursuit

John Piper wrote in *Don't Waste Your Life* that "God created me—and you—to live with a single, all-embracing, all-transforming passion—namely, a passion to glorify God by enjoying and displaying his supreme excellence in all the spheres of life"[4] How do we enjoy and display his supreme excellence? By pursuing. Nothing holds us back, holds us down, or keeps us too long that we give up pursuing Christ. At the center of our attention is our pursuit of Christ. This is daily. It is changing me. It is changing you. Christ is calling to you above all the noise of the world to pursue him. Because you are intent on listening to him you hear him. My childhood best friend could play for as long as she wanted until she would hear her mother's whistle. That whistle could be heard no matter where we were in our neighborhood. My friend would hear it, stop, and go back to her house. Why? There was no distraction that was more important than the signal of that whistle.

As you and I pursue our Lord in the middle of our darkest days and confusing times, we will recognize him above all else. When we live with a passion that is singly focused on the One we were made for, others notice. They don't always understand it all. However,

4   John Piper, *Don't Waste Your Life* (Crossway Books, 2003), 31.

the person who is actively pursuing the Lord will be a magnet to others. People discover that she is less concerned with the details of a crisis and more in tune to knowing the God holding her together. Christ works loudly with the person who pursues him. Be ready. Your authentic life will be noticed and you will be able to lead a pursuit that is worthy of a great calling—the calling to honor the Lord Jesus with your life.

Intentional Walk

Pursuing Christ has to be intentional. You can't stumble into a life in Christ. You become deliberate in all that you do for the Lord as you walk with him through your crisis. There is one primary focus of the one being intentional, and when we are being deliberate in this then everything else will fall into place. "Jesus answered, 'The most important is…'" you shall love the Lord your God with all your heart and with all your soul and with all your mind and with all your strength." The second is this: "You shall love your neighbor as yourself." There is no other commandment greater than these'" (Mark 12:29–31, ESV). This is what you and I focus on as we rebuild. This is what the Lord commands us to do as we are being restored. Deitrich Bonhoeffer said it best in this well-known quotation: "Being a Christian is less about cautiously avoiding sin than about courageously and actively doing God's will."

If we are not careful we can easily turn intentionality into a list of do's and don'ts. As we live our life loving the Lord with everything, we will find living for him far outweighs living for ourselves. His desires become our desires. We are very sensitive to sin in our life. We become more discerning to Satan's deceptions. We do become courageous about doing God's will. If you and I intentionally love Christ with all of our heart, mind, soul, and strength then we have the perfect blueprint to rebuild, a simple blueprint with complex implications. Our credibility for being effective hangs in the balance. In Christ we are given credibility because our identity is in him. However, to affect others we must live with great intention to love the Lord and love others. To emerge from our crisis filled with bitterness, anger, resentment, and an undisciplined lifestyle will discredit us to others. To emerge from our crisis loving the Lord with all of our heart, soul, mind, strength, and loving others as ourselves will give great credibility. We will be made credible by the One we are living for. The One we live for will give us the deep desire to love. When you and I emerge from our crisis filled with great love for God and others, people will be affected.

Contagious Faith

Only one of my second grade classmates had to be contagious with the chicken pox to infect the rest of our class. We can be that one person who begins to expose others with the love of God. It is simple. We make it difficult. If we are not careful we will keep to ourselves, perhaps thinking we cannot share what Christ has done and is doing in our life because certain things have not fallen into place. I struggled with this. The lies Satan will tell you might seem to make sense. I went through several months thinking I was useless. I really wondered whether God was through with me. Like the chicken pox virus, we can be contagious even when it may not be completely evident to the outside world. Just as there are no outward signs of chicken pox at first, your life hidden in Christ (at least while we withstand the devastating blows of crisis) may reveal no immediate outward signs. Hold on! You will be restored and as Christ restores you there will be evidence of your contagious faith. When the spots begin to show, the chicken pox virus is nearing the end. However, our contagious faith being made known to others is only the beginning for a transformed, Spirit-filled life.

"And I am sure of this, that he who began a good work in you will bring it to completion at the day of Jesus Christ" (Philippians 1:6, ESV). Friend, please don't go through your crisis thinking that one day you will "arrive." You won't, at least not on this side of Heaven. Take heart; the Lord begins a good work in you when you choose to follow Christ. Your faith begins as a quiet surrender and as time moves along you become contagious. The heart changed by Christ will expose others to that change by the outward signs of living for the Lord. What would our lives be like if others placed themselves in our proximity because they wanted to be exposed to the truth and love of the almighty God? What would happen if every person we came into contact with realized we had something that they needed? Our life in crisis is considered a joy that will intrigue others to know more about the One who is our strength.

After the wall was rebuilt and the gates were hung, the people sealed a covenant with the Lord. "…to observe and do all the commandments of the LORD our Lord and his rules and his statutes" (Nehemiah 10:29b, ESV). When we commit to honor the Lord and follow his ways regardless of how messy our crisis has been, he will expose his great love through us. Not only did the people at Jerusalem commit to follow the Lord's commands; they also gave thanks. "And they offered great sacrifices that day and rejoiced, for God had made them rejoice with great joy; the women and children also rejoiced. And the joy of Jerusalem was heard far away" (Nehemiah 12:43). Another translation reads, "…because God had given them great joy" (NASB). I can say that even though my crisis has broken my heart in more pieces than I can count and left me with wounds that are still tender, he has given me great joy. What a gift. The Israelites not only were given great joy but their joy was heard from far away. We too have been given a great joy and we should declare it. This is what happens when our credibility is in Christ. Others know about you. They may not know the details of your crisis or all the tears that have accompanied you as you have done the hard work of rebuilding. What they will know and want to know is the joy that you cannot suppress.

Scripture References

About the Author

 Joy McHale, a native of Warner Robins, Georgia, holds a Bachelor of Science in Counseling and a certification in sex and relationship addiction. She attended Liberty University in Lynchburg, Virginia, and Toccoa Falls College in Toccoa, Georgia. Joy served as staff counselor at Southside Baptist Church in Warner Robins for seven years before joining Snowbird's staff in May 2012. As ministry counselor, Joy oversees student-counseling sessions and meets one-on-one with students for intensive, focused encouragement and direction. In addition to her work at Snowbird, she often speaks at women's conferences, encouraging women to disconnect from worldly distractions and surrender to Christ. Joy is the single mother of two children: Meighan and Caid.

CPSIA information can be obtained at www.ICGtesting.com
Printed in the USA
BVOW08s0433310114

343203BV00001B/3/P